Rachel's IRISH FAMILY FOOD

A collection of Rachel's best-loved family recipes

RACHEL ALLEN

641.59415

Rachel's
IRISH FAMILY FOOD

Contents

Introduction

This is a cookbook I have always wanted to write. It's a collection of my very best family recipes, seriously comforting and nourishing food, all inspired by both traditional and modern Irish cooking. In Ireland we have fabulous ingredient-led dishes that make the most of the incredible produce from our farms and fish and seafood from our coast. These are my favourite recipes to cook for my family, the ones I turn to again and again. Whether or not you're familiar with Irish food, I'm sure you'll love this celebration of our country's culinary culture.

Irish food has a rich history and tradition. Of course, our love for the potato is well known and very real, but with recipes such as colcannon, Irish stew and our wonderful soda bread there are so many distinctively Irish dishes that make our food ideal for home-cooked meals – wherever in the world you might live. I grew up in Dublin and my mum was a very good cook. She would often have casseroles gently bubbling in the oven, filling the kitchen with their alluring aromas to make my sister and me ever more impatiently hungry.

My own relationship with cooking started with baking. My sister, mother and I would often bake together, making biscuits or cakes. I loved the whole process, from the messy mixing to the mysterious rise behind the oven door. It was at the age of eighteen that my interest in cooking became a passion and eventually an obsession. I travelled down to East Cork to study at the famous Ballymaloe Cookery School, which at the time had been going for six years, and at which I still teach to this day. It was at the cooking school that I met its founder, Darina Allen, who would eventually become my mother-in-law! I also met her mother-in-law, Myrtle Allen, the matriarch of Irish food who had founded the Ballymaloe House Restaurant and guest house all the way back in 1964.

On my first day at the cooking school I learned many of the principles that we still teach students today: that the best food comes from the best ingredients and that means carefully grown crops and lovingly raised animals. The school sits in the middle of an organic farm from which we get the students' cooking ingredients. It opened my eyes to how much more important proper produce is than complicated or long-winded recipes.

This is echoed by our impressive and still rapidly expanding modern Irish food culture. Ours is not a history of elaborate multilayered dishes. Irish food is about local produce. The greenest grass in the world feeds the happiest cows, which in turn produce the most beautiful butter and cheeses. We have teams of small dedicated farmers who put their efforts into growing delectable crops and our cold water creates the sweetest seafood. With ingredients like this, I think it's important not to dress up the food too much, to let their flavours take centre stage. This book is filled with simple and easily achievable dishes that I love to cook and, perhaps most importantly, that I love to eat!

The recipes range from light suppers for a summer's evening to big hearty casseroles for when the wind is blowing and the rain is lashing down. There are everyday dinners for school nights when you've been at work all day, as well as slightly more involved recipes when you want to make something a little more special. All the recipes are easy to follow and not at all difficult to execute.

I've also included four passages about each of the different provinces in Ireland, with information about the food as well as the people, their history and folklore. Irish culture is ancient but alive and vibrant, with food a fundamental piece of it. I hope that through our food you can connect both to the history of Ireland and to the wonderful country that it still is today.

Soups and light meals

These are the sorts of dishes I like to serve as a casual supper or a light lunch. They are versatile recipes and not too filling. A soup, for example, can easily feed a family if accompanied by lots of delicious crusty bread. Probably due in no small part to our blustery and bracing weather, there is a real tradition of warming soups in Ireland. It might be a nourishing broth such as the West Cork Broth with Gubbeen Bacon (page 43) or a rich and creamy comforting soup like the two different chowder recipes in this chapter.

Lots of the recipes in this chapter would also work really well as an starter for a larger meal. Asparagus with Hollandaise Sauce (page 12) is one of my absolute favourites when made with perfect Irish butter from our greenest pastures. It makes the most divine supper on its own, but if you're having guests over, then a few asparagus spears cooked this way is a lovely way to begin a meal. The same is true of the wonderful combination of fresh oysters with a glass of Guinness (page 25).

Asparagus on toast with hollandaise sauce

Vegetarian

Serves 4

Preparation time: 5 minutes

Cooking time: 20 minutes

16–20 asparagus spears

Good pinch of salt

A few slices of Brown Soda Bread (page 227)

Butter

Hollandaise sauce (see below)

Asparagus has to be my favourite vegetable. The exquisitely flavoured bright green spears have a season that is always sadly short. Ireland has perfect growing conditions to produce some of the best asparagus I've ever tasted. There are lots of different ways of cooking and serving asparagus, but to me this is the very best: simply boiled in salted water and served on Brown Soda Bread (page 227) with butter and lashings of hollandaise sauce.

Snap off the tough woody end of each asparagus stalk and discard. Fill a large saucepan to a depth of 4–6cm (1½–2½in) with water, add the salt and bring to a boil. Tip in the asparagus and cook in the boiling water for 4–8 minutes, until tender when pierced with a sharp knife. Drain immediately.

While the asparagus is cooking, toast the bread, then spread with the butter and remove the crusts, if you wish. For each person, place a piece of toast on a warmed plate, put 4–5 asparagus spears on top and spoon over a little hollandaise sauce.

Hollandaise sauce

Vegetarian

Makes 75ml (3fl oz)

Preparation time: 5 minutes

Cooking time: 5 minutes

1 egg yolk

1 tbsp cold water

50g (2oz) butter, diced

Freshly squeezed lemon juice

Salt and freshly ground black pepper

Place a heatproof bowl over a saucepan of simmering water over medium heat. (The water must not boil to avoid heating the sauce so much it scrambles or curdles; take the pan off the heat every so often.) Add the egg yolk and cold water. Whisking all the time, gradually add the butter, a few pieces at a time, until each addition has melted and emulsified before adding the next.

Once all the butter has been incorporated, season to taste with lemon juice and salt and pepper, if necessary. Remove from the heat and serve immediately or leave to sit over the warm water until you're ready to serve.

Artichokes with melted butter

Vegetarian

Serves 6

Preparation time: 5 minutes

Cooking time: 30 minutes

6 globe artichokes

Salt

White wine vinegar

175g (6oz) butter

Juice of ½ lemon, freshly squeezed, plus extra for dipping

Globe artichokes have been grown in the gardens of Irish country houses such as Ballymaloe for years. They make a beautiful plant, tall and proud, but it is their bright purple thistle-like flower heads that cooks prize. This is my favourite way of serving them. No olive oil here, only simply boiled artichokes and perfect Irish butter. I love the quiet methodical way one eats artichokes. To eat them, pull away each leaf from the artichoke, dip in the butter, then put the leaf in your mouth and scrape off the flesh from the base with your teeth. Discard that leaf and pick another. Eventually you'll get down to the yellow choke: Scrape this off and discard to reveal the tender and juicy heart.

Just before cooking, trim the base of the artichokes so they will sit steadily on the plate. Dip the cut end in lemon juice to prevent it from discolouring.

Fill a saucepan large enough to hold all of the artichokes three-quarters full with water. Add 2 teaspoons salt and 2 teaspoons white wine vinegar for every litre (1¾ pints) of water. Bring to a boil over high heat.

Carefully add the artichokes (they should be completely covered with water). Bring back to a boil, then reduce the heat to medium and simmer for about 25 minutes, until the larger leaves at the base of the plant come away easily if you pull on them. If they don't, then continue to cook for another 5–10 minutes. When cooked, remove the artichokes from the water and drain upside down on a plate.

While the artichokes cook, heat the butter in a saucepan over medium–low heat just until melted, then stir in the lemon juice, transfer to a few serving bowls and set aside.

To serve, remove the tough outer leaves and discard. Place each artichoke, while still warm, onto a serving plate. Either give each person their own serving bowl of butter or have the bowls within easy reach.

Dublin bay prawns with mayonnaise

Serves 4–6

Preparation time: 5 minutes

Cooking time: 5 minutes

4.8 litres (8½ pints) water

4 tbsp salt

1kg (2lb 2oz) Dublin bay prawns with heads on, or any large prawns

Mayonnaise (see below), to serve

The divine sweetness of Dublin bay prawns (also known as langoustines) is a result of our cold waters, and I love to eat them simply, with just a little mayonnaise, either plain or with a few herbs stirred through.

Fill a large saucepan with the water, add the salt and bring to a boil over high heat. When the water is at a good rolling boil, add the prawns. Return the water to a boil and cook for 2–3 minutes, depending on their size. The best way to tell when prawns are cooked is to take one from the pan once they rise to the top of the water, after a minute or so of boiling. If it is opaque and firm all the way through, then they are ready to drain.

As soon as the prawns are cooked, drain and lay them out to cool on flat trays to keep them from cooking any further.

Serve at room temperature with a bowl of mayonnaise on the side.

Mayonnaise

Vegetarian

Makes 300ml (11fl oz)

Preparation time: 5 minutes

2 egg yolks

Pinch of salt

1 tsp Dijon mustard

2 tsp white wine vinegar

200ml (7fl oz) sunflower oil

25ml (1fl oz) extra virgin olive oil

Freshly ground black pepper

2 tbsp chopped fresh herbs (chives, dill, fennel) (optional)

Put the egg yolks in a bowl and mix in the salt, mustard and vinegar.

Mix the sunflower oil and the extra virgin olive oil in a jug.

Very gradually, whisking all the time (either by hand or using a hand-held electric beater), slowly pour the oil into the bowl in a very thin stream. You should see the mixture start to thicken. Keep whisking and adding the oil slowly until it has all been incorporated. Season with pepper and more salt to taste. Stir in the chopped herbs (if using).

Ivan Allen's dressed crab

Serves 6

Preparation time: 15 minutes
(plus 45 minutes to prep crabs)

Cooking time: 20 minutes
(plus 40 minutes to cook crabs)

425g (15oz) meat from 3–4 cooked
fresh large crabs, reserving the
crab shells

200g (7oz) soft white breadcrumbs

150ml (5fl oz) Basic White Sauce
(page 114)

2 tbsp Tomato Relish (page 20)

2 tsp white wine vinegar

1 tsp Dijon mustard, or a generous
pinch of dry mustard powder

75g (3oz) butter, melted

Salt and freshly ground black
pepper

FOR THE TOMATO AND BASIL SALAD

8 vine-ripened tomatoes (using one
variety or a mixture)

Salt and freshly ground black
pepper

Pinch of sugar

Juice from a good squeeze of lemon

2–3 tbsp extra virgin olive oil

Small handful of basil leaves, larger
leaves torn

Ivan Allen was Isaac's grandfather, and this is his recipe. I remember him coming into the kitchens at Ballymaloe and checking the dressed crab whenever it was on the menu to ensure it was just right. If you are using brown crabs, try to find whole crabs so that you can use both the white and flavourful brown meat. I've given instructions for cooking a crab from scratch, but if you can't get hold of a whole crab, you can use ready-cooked fresh or frozen crabmeat instead. For serving you will need two or three crab shells or six 250ml (9fl oz) ramekins or small dishes.

Preheat the oven to 180°C/350°F/Gas Mark 4. If you plan to serve from the crab shells, scrub them clean, dry well and arrange upside down on a baking tray. Alternatively, place six 250ml (9fl oz) ramekins or small dishes on the baking tray.

In a large bowl, mix together the crabmeat, just over three-quarters of the breadcrumbs, the white sauce, relish, vinegar, mustard and 2 tablespoons of the melted butter; season to taste with salt and pepper. Spoon the mixture into the crab shells or ramekins. In a separate bowl, toss together the remaining breadcrumbs with the remaining butter and sprinkle over the crab mixture.

Bake for 15–20 minutes, until heated through and browned on top. Briefly place under a preheated grill, if necessary, to crisp up the crumbs.

In the meantime, prepare the salad. Cut the tomatoes into quarters or 1cm (½in) slices. Spread out in a single layer on a large flat plate and season to taste with salt, pepper and sugar. Drizzle over the lemon juice, then the extra virgin olive oil; scatter the basil leaves over. Toss together gently.

Serve the baked crab with the tomato salad and some fresh crusty bread on the side.

How to cook a crab
First place the crab in the freezer for a couple of hours so that it is unconscious before boiling. Place the frozen crab in a large saucepan, cover with warm water, add 1 tablespoon of salt for every 1.2 litres (2 pints) of water and bring to a boil. Simmer over medium heat for

recipe continues overleaf

20 minutes for every 450g (1lb). Pour off about two-thirds of the water, cover with a lid and continue to cook for another 6 minutes. To see if the crab is cooked, gently shake it quite close to your ear; you shouldn't hear liquid splashing around. If you do hear water, the crab isn't quite cooked and will need another few minutes. Remove the crab from the water and allow to cool.

To remove the meat, first remove the large claws and crack these (using a heavy weight or nut crackers), then extract every bit of meat using the handle of a teaspoon. Turn the body of the crab upside down and pull out the centre portion. Discard the gills, known as 'dead man's fingers', each about 4cm (1½in) long. Scoop out all the lovely brown meat from the body and add it to the meat from the claws. The meat can be used immediately or frozen for future use. Retain the shell if making dressed crab, otherwise discard.

Tomato relish

Vegetarian

Makes 1 x 300ml (11fl oz) jar

Preparation time: 5 minutes

Cooking time: 2 hours

---

1 x 400g (14oz) can chopped tomatoes

1 onion, finely chopped

200ml (7fl oz) white wine vinegar

130g (4½oz) caster or granulated sugar

100g (3½oz) sultanas or raisins

4 tbsp water

1 tsp wholegrain mustard

1 tsp tomato purée

½ tsp ground cumin

½ tsp ground coriander

Pinch of ground cloves

A really useful relish recipe, this is my version of Ballymaloe's famous Country Relish. It works with many different foods, from cold meats and sausages to cheese sandwiches and dressed crab.

Combine all ingredients in a saucepan over low heat. Bring to a simmer and continue to cook on a low simmer, stirring occasionally, for about 1½ hours, until a slightly reduced chunky consistency. Use immediately or store in an airtight jar in the fridge for up to 2 months.

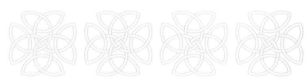

Mussels with garlic and breadcrumbs

Serves 4–6

Preparation time: 10 minutes

Cooking time: 10 minutes

900g (2lb) mussels in their shells,
  scrubbed clean

50g (2oz) butter

50g (2oz) fresh white breadcrumbs
  (see tip below)

1 large clove garlic, crushed
  or grated

1 tbsp chopped fresh parsley

These are a retro favourite, beloved of Irish restaurants in the eighties. When done right, they're absolutely fantastic: crisp crunchy breadcrumbs atop plump mussels. Mussels, one of the least expensive of shellfish, grow freely on our shores and have long fed the people of the coast. They're such good value, and I love that they're so quick to cook. Serve with bread or toast to mop up all the juices.

Check over the mussels and, if any are open, give them a tap; if they don't close, discard them. Put the tightly shut mussels with just 1 tablespoon of water in a large saucepan over low heat and cover with the lid. They will open in the steam. If you catch them when they are just opening, they will be delicious and juicy, so don't overcook them. Remove the mussels from the pan (keeping any juices for a fish soup, pie, stew or even to mix with mayonnaise served with shellfish such as prawns). Discard any cooked mussels with unopened shells.

Discard half a shell from each mussel and pull out the beard – the little fibrous tuft – from the straight side of each mussel.

Melt the butter in a medium saucepan over medium–low heat. Add the breadcrumbs, garlic and parsley and mix together. With a spoon, firmly pack the breadcrumb mixture on top of each mussel. Place the mussels, crumb side up, in a single layer on ovenproof plates or gratin dishes. (These can be prepared up to 24 hours in advance.) When you are ready to eat, pop them under a preheated grill until golden, crunchy and bubbly, 1–2 minutes.

Variations

While it isn't classically Irish, sometimes I feel like adding a bit more zip to this recipe, so in place of the parsley, I add 1 tablespoon chopped fresh coriander together with one-quarter to one-half of a fresh red chilli, deseeded and chopped. Or you could try adding some grated lemon zest to the crumbs.

Rachel's tip

To make breadcrumbs, place slices of white bread (with or without the crusts) in a food processor, and whiz until you have crumbs, about 20 seconds.

Oysters with Guinness

Serves 4

Preparation time: 30 minutes

24 oysters (opened in their shells)

A glass of Guinness each, to serve

Lemon wedges, pepper or Tabasco sauce, to serve (optional)

Once considered a food for the peasants, oysters are now a prized delicacy. There is nothing quite like the salty, creamy flesh that tastes so much of the sea. In Ireland, oysters are always shucked to order and they are celebrated at oyster festivals across the country with shucking competitions and various oyster-based events.

Oysters need little accompaniment; some people like a few grinds of pepper or drops of Tabasco or lemon. It's up to you, though I like the pure unadulterated oyster flavour and have mine on their own. Stout and oysters go particularly well with each other, and the two served together is a quintessentially Irish dish. For a more celebratory drink, you could make Black Velvets, made by adding two parts stout to one part Champagne. Both my husband Isaac and I adore Black Velvets whether with oysters or without, and we served them at midnight at our wedding.

How to open an oyster

It is best to use an oyster knife, which is designed for the purpose and will make your life much easier (and safer). If you don't have an oyster knife, you can use a thin chisel, but do not attempt to open oysters with any knife that has a bendy blade.

Fold a tea towel lengthways and wrap it around your hand once or twice to protect it. Place the oyster on the remaining edge of the towel, with the flatter side of the oyster facing up. You will see a slight crevice where the shells meet at the narrow end.

Take your oyster knife (or thin clean chisel) and insert the blade into the crevice while holding the opposite end steady with your wrapped hand. Press and turn the knife, levering upwards. Once the shell pops open, insert a clean knife just under the top shell to cut the oyster away; it will suddenly become free.

Cut the membrane where the oyster is attached to the shell and remove the oyster altogether or replace it on the shell, discarding any bits of broken shell. Serve immediately, if possible, or store in the fridge in a sealed container until serving.

Smoked mackerel pâté

Serves 4–6

Preparation time: 15 minutes

Cooking time: 15–20 minutes

1 large fillet smoked mackerel
(about 100g/3½oz)

75g (3oz) cream cheese, softened

75g (3oz) crème fraîche or sour
cream

Juice of ½ lemon

Salt and freshly ground black
pepper

This is one of my favourite quick recipes, as impressive as it is quick to put together. I love having some of this in my fridge for a snack or a packed lunch, and it will keep there for a week. The better the smoked mackerel you use the better your pâté will be. I sometimes serve this on slices of Brown Soda Bread (page 227) with Cucumber Pickle (page 133). For a family meal I like to serve this pâté as a starter, in a bowl in the centre of the table with lots of crusty bread or toast to go around. That way everyone can dig in while the rest of the meal is being prepared.

In a food processor, whiz the smoked mackerel. Add the cream cheese and the crème fraîche or sour cream and whiz just until smooth. Empty into a bowl and fold in the lemon juice, salt and pepper to taste.

Chicken livers with bacon and sage

Serves 2–4

Preparation time: 10 minutes

Cooking time: 15 minutes

2 tbsp extra virgin olive oil

150g (5oz) bacon, cut into 2cm (¾in) pieces

1 clove garlic, sliced

300g (11oz) chicken livers, green parts removed

Salt and freshly ground black pepper

1–2 tbsp chopped fresh sage

2 tbsp marsala, port or brandy

4 tbsp single cream (optional)

I adore chicken livers for their soft texture and rich flavour. Chicken livers are less popular in Ireland than they used to be, when people would make sure to eat every part of the animal. Chicken livers and crispy bacon is a classic combination and makes a divine starter with some crusty bread, or serve as a supper with Creamy Mashed Potato (page 166).

Add 1 tablespoon of the olive oil to a frying pan over medium heat. Add the bacon and fry for a few minutes until golden, then transfer onto kitchen paper to drain, then set aside.

Add the remaining 1 tablespoon of olive oil and the garlic and fry for 1–2 minutes, until slightly golden.

Add the chicken livers, season with salt and pepper and cook the livers for 2–3 minutes on each side, until they're browned on the outside but still a little pink in the middle.

Add the reserved bacon, sage and marsala. Increase the heat and bubble for just 30 seconds (be careful as the alcohol may flame) then remove from the heat.

If you'd like a creamier dish, leave the pan over high heat, add the cream and allow it to bubble for 30 seconds or so.

Season to taste and serve immediately.

Chicken livers with onions

Serves 2

Preparation time: 10 minutes

Cooking time: 30 minutes

25g (1oz) butter

2 onions, thinly sliced

300g (11oz) chicken livers

Salt and freshly ground black pepper

2 tbsp dry sherry

100ml (3½fl oz) Chicken Stock (page 35) or Vegetable Stock (page 34)

The Irish have always believed it is important to eat the whole animal. Livers or kidneys are often served alongside our beloved potatoes, which may be simply boiled or in a creamy mash. This is a more modern version of a dish my grandmother used to make a lot. The dry sherry gives the dish real depth; you could also use brandy, port or even white wine. If you have time, make some Creamy Mashed Potato (page 166) to accompany them. Otherwise make sure to mop up every last drop with some good crusty bread.

Melt 1 tablespoon of the butter in a frying pan over medium–high heat and, when foaming, add the onions. Fry, stirring occasionally, for 15–20 minutes, until the onions are completely soft and golden. Tip the onions onto a plate and set aside.

Season the chicken livers with salt and pepper. Melt the remaining butter in the pan over medium–high heat. When the butter starts to foam, add the chicken livers and cook for 2– 4 minutes on each side, until browned on the outside but still a little pink in the middle.

Add the sherry and allow it to bubble for 30 seconds. Add the cooked onions and stock. Stir together, bring to a boil, then reduce the heat to medium–low and cook for 1–2 minutes, until the stock has slightly reduced. Serve immediately.

Field mushroom soup

Vegetarian (if using vegetable stock)

Serves 6

Preparation time: 10 minutes

Cooking time: 40 minutes

25g (1oz) butter

1 onion, finely chopped

2 cloves garlic, finely chopped

350g (12oz) large flat field mushrooms, quartered

1 tbsp chopped fresh thyme

Salt and freshly ground black pepper

600ml (1 pint) Chicken Stock (page 35) or Vegetable Stock (page 34)

150ml (5fl oz) double or whipping cream

1 tbsp finely chopped fresh chives

Mushroom soup is an easy family favourite, rich and velvety with a lovely texture because it isn't puréed. From the mountains of Wicklow to the woodlands of Kerry, we have an abundance of great wild and farmed mushrooms in Ireland. I use large flat field mushrooms when I can because they have a better flavour than the smaller button mushrooms.

Melt the butter in a large saucepan over medium heat. Add the onion and garlic and cook for 8–10 minutes, until softened and slightly golden.

Finely chop the mushrooms in the food processor or by hand and add the mushrooms to the saucepan along with the thyme. Place over medium–low heat, cover and cook for about 5 minutes or until softened. Season with salt and pepper. Pour in the stock and bring slowly to a boil; then reduce the heat and simmer gently for 25 minutes.

Pour in the cream and simmer gently for a few minutes, then stir in the chives and serve immediately.

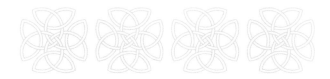

Vegetable stock

Vegetarian

Makes about 2 litres (3½ pints)

Preparation time: 10 minutes

Cooking time: 1 hour

2 onions, roughly chopped

2 leeks, trimmed and roughly chopped

3 celery stalks, trimmed and roughly chopped

3 carrots, roughly chopped

½ fennel bulb, roughly chopped

Bunch of parsley stems

1 small sprig of rosemary

1 sprig of thyme

Water

A really useful stock, perfect for vegetarians or when you don't want a meaty flavour in your dish.

Combine the onions, leeks, celery, carrots, fennel, parsley, rosemary and thyme in a large saucepan. Add enough cold water to cover the ingredients by about 10cm (4in) and bring to a simmer. Continue to simmer for an hour, then strain the liquid and discard the vegetables.

Chicken stock

Makes about 2 litres (3½ pints)

Preparation time: 5 minutes

Cooking time: 2 hours

1 chicken carcass (either raw or cooked)

1 onion, unpeeled and halved, or 1 leek, split and halved

1–2 carrots, halved lengthways

1 celery stalk

1 small bay leaf

1 sprig of parsley

1 sprig of thyme

4 peppercorns

3 litres (5¼ pints) water

Salt and freshly ground black pepper

Chicken stock is invaluable, forming the basis for so many stews, sauces and soups. Homemade chicken stock, with its intense, fresh flavour, is best of all. Indeed, making stock is a very good way of using up ingredients that might otherwise be thrown away – onion peel, carrot and celery trimmings and, of course, chicken bones. Get into the habit of making stock whenever you have a chicken carcass on hand – whether cooked or raw. If you're not using the stock straight away, it will store in the fridge for 2–3 days, or you can pour it into several small containers to freeze.

Combine the chicken carcass, onion, carrots, celery, bay leaf, parsley, thyme and peppercorns in a large saucepan. Add the water and bring to a boil. Reduce the heat and simmer over medium heat, covered but with a wooden spoon between the lid and the pan to allow the steam to escape, for about 2 hours, until you have a well-flavoured stock.

Strain the stock through a fine sieve into a large bowl or jug, discarding the bits in the sieve. Allow to cool, skimming off any fat from the surface of the stock as it cools.

Ballycotton fish chowder

Serves 4

Preparation time: 15 minutes

Cooking time: 15–20 minutes

Extra virgin olive oil

100g (3½oz) bacon, cut into 1cm (½in) dice

1 small onion, chopped

Salt and freshly ground black pepper

175g (6oz) potatoes, peeled and cut into 1cm (½in) cubes

500ml (18fl oz) Chicken Stock (page 35)

350ml (12fl oz) milk

Pinch of cayenne pepper

200g (7oz) fish fillets (mixture of salmon and a white fish, such as pollock, haddock or cod) cut into 2–3cm (¾–1in) chunks

100g (3½oz) smoked haddock or smoked salmon, cut into 2cm (¾in) pieces

1 tbsp chopped fresh chives

1 tbsp chopped fresh parsley

Ballycotton is our local fishing village, and nearly all the fish we eat and cook here at the Ballymaloe Cookery School comes from there. Ireland's long coastline gives a glorious abundance of the very best fish, and chowder is a much-loved staple on pub, café and restaurant menus throughout the coast. The best of the local fish goes into this rich and creamy soup. I always make chowder using some smoked fish because I love the way that smokiness flavours the whole bowl. You can also add some whole mussels in their shells (be sure to discard any that remain closed after cooking).

Serve with Brown Soda Bread (page 227), Wholemeal Honey Bread (page 233) or Brown Yeast Bread (page 230).

Pour a small drizzle of olive oil into a large saucepan over medium heat. When the oil is hot, tip in the bacon. Fry for 4–5 minutes, stirring occasionally, until all the fat has rendered and the bacon is crispy and golden brown.

Add the onion, season with salt and pepper (bearing in mind that the bacon is quite salty) and cook for another 5 minutes. Then add the potatoes with the stock, milk and cayenne.

Bring to a boil, reduce the heat and simmer for 3 minutes, or until the cubes of potato are half cooked. Add the fish and gently simmer for another 3–4 minutes, until the fish is opaque and the potatoes are tender. Season with salt and pepper to taste, stir in the chopped herbs and serve.

Molly Malone's cockle and mussel chowder

Serves 4–6

Preparation time: 10 minutes

Cooking time: 20 minutes

2 tbsp sunflower oil

110g (4oz) smoked bacon, diced

25g (1oz) butter

110g (4oz) leek, trimmed and very finely diced

110g (4oz) carrot, very finely diced

275g (10oz) potato (about 1 medium), peeled and finely diced

1kg (2lb 2oz) mixed cockles and mussels

300ml (11fl oz) dry white wine

200ml (7fl oz) milk

200ml (7fl oz) single or double cream

Salt and freshly ground black pepper

4 tbsp roughly chopped fresh parsley

Molly Malone was a beautiful girl who sold cockles and mussels and died tragically of a fever while still young, or so the song goes. Molly may not have been a real girl, but since at least the 17th century, there have been fishmongers on the streets of Dublin who sell 'Cockles and Mussels, alive, alive, oh!'

Cockles, with their distinctive flavour and lovely curved shell, are traditionally eaten in Ireland with Oatcakes (page 248). If you can only find mussels, this chowder will be just as good.

Serve either as a substantial starter or with chunks of crusty bread as a meal in its own right.

Heat the sunflower oil in a saucepan over medium-high heat. Add the bacon and sauté for about 1 minute, until crisp and golden. Add the butter to the pan and melt. Then add the leek, carrot and potato. Reduce the heat to low and sauté gently for 4–5 minutes, until soft but not browned.

Meanwhile, prepare the cockles and mussels. Scrub the shells clean and discard any that remain open when you tap them against a hard surface. Remove the beard – the little fibrous tuft – from each mussel. Bring the wine to a boil in a large saucepan and add the cockles and mussels. Cover with a tight-fitting lid and cook for 3–4 minutes, shaking the pan occasionally, until the shells have opened.

Remove from the heat, drain the shellfish in a colander, reserving the cooking juices, and discard any shells that remain closed. Return the shellfish to the empty pan to keep warm. Place a fine sieve over a measuring jug and strain the cooking liquid. You should have at least 600ml (1 pint); if not, add water to make up that quantity.

Add the pan juices and the milk to the bacon and vegetable mixture and bring to a boil. Reduce the heat and simmer for 6–8 minutes, until the potato is tender. Add the cream and simmer for another 2–3 minutes, until the soup is reduced and thickened slightly. Season with salt and pepper.

Meanwhile, remove half of the cockles and mussels from their shells and add them with the remaining cockles and mussels still in their shells to the chowder. Stir in the parsley and serve at once.

West Cork broth with Gubbeen bacon

Serves 6

Preparation time: 15 minutes

Cooking time: 25 minutes

250g (9oz) unsmoked, unsliced Gubbeen bacon (rind removed) or pancetta, cut into 1cm (½in) cubes

2 tbsp olive or sunflower oil

150g (5oz) potatoes, peeled and cut into 5mm (¼in) dice

1 medium onion, finely chopped

2 celery stalks, finely chopped

2 cloves garlic, crushed or finely grated

450g (1lb) tomatoes, peeled and diced, or 1 x 400g (14oz) can chopped tomatoes

Salt and freshly ground black pepper

1 tsp sugar

850ml (1½ pints) Chicken Stock (page 35)

50g (2oz) finely shredded kale or savoy cabbage

2 tbsp chopped fresh flat-leaf parsley

This is a comforting, restorative broth – warming and nourishing in equal measure. It uses unsliced bacon, which is sadly becoming increasingly uncommon in many places outside of Ireland. It works so well in this dish, because the bacon is cut into cubes that have just the right amount of juicy meatiness. It uses unsmoked bacon, or 'green' bacon. If you can't find unsmoked bacon, use pancetta.

I like to use Gubbeen bacon; their farm in West Cork has deliciously happy pigs, and they also make one of my favourite Irish cheeses.

Bring a saucepan of water to a boil over high heat. Add the bacon cubes and cook for 1 minute. Drain and dry on kitchen paper.

Heat the oil in a large saucepan over medium heat. Add the bacon and fry for 3–5 minutes until crisp and golden; then add the potatoes, onion, celery and garlic. Reduce the heat to medium–low, cover and cook for 10 minutes, stirring occasionally. Stir in the tomatoes and season with salt, pepper and sugar.

Add the stock and bring to a simmer. Cook for 5 minutes, stir in the kale, and simmer for a minute or so, until just tender. Taste for seasoning, sprinkle with the parsley and serve.

Potato, leek and smoked bacon soup

Serves 6

Preparation time: 15 minutes

Cooking time: 15 minutes

1 tbsp sunflower or olive oil

4 rashers smoked bacon, diced

25g (1oz) butter

1 onion, roughly chopped

1 large leek, trimmed and diced

2 large potatoes (about 450g/1lb in total)

Salt and freshly ground black pepper

1.2 litres (2 pints) Chicken Stock (page 35) or Vegetable Stock (page 34)

FOR THE PARSLEY PESTO

15g (½oz) fresh flat-leaf parsley

1 clove garlic, roughly chopped

1 tbsp pine nuts, lightly toasted

1 tbsp finely grated Parmesan cheese

4 tbsp extra virgin olive oil, plus more if needed

Salt and freshly ground black pepper

A soup made from the kind of staples that few Irish kitchens are ever without, with the potatoes forming the basis of a rustic and substantial meal in a bowl. The smoky flavour from the bacon gives this soup magnificent depth. Parsley pesto is an updated version of what many years ago would have been simply chopped parsley. It speaks to a modern Ireland, with its international influences.

This soup is great served with Brown Soda Bread (page 227).

Heat the oil in a large saucepan over high heat, add the bacon, and sauté for about 1 minute, or until crisp and golden. Remove from the pan and drain on kitchen paper.

Reduce the heat a little and add the butter to the oil in the pan. When it has melted, add the onion, leek and potatoes. Season with salt and pepper and cook gently for 8–10 minutes without browning. Pour in the stock and simmer gently for 5 minutes, or until the potatoes are completely cooked through.

Meanwhile, make the parsley pesto. Discard the stems from the parsley and put the leaves in a bowl with the garlic, pine nuts, Parmesan and olive oil. Using a hand-held blender, purée to a fairly smooth paste, adding a little more oil, if necessary, so that it is a thick but drizzling consistency. Alternatively, crush the parsley, garlic and pine nuts using a pestle and mortar and stir in the Parmesan and olive oil. Season to taste with salt and pepper and set aside.

Purée the soup until smooth in a blender or using a hand-held blender. Return to the pan and stir in all but 1 tablespoon of the reserved bacon pieces. Check the seasoning, adjusting if necessary, and heat for a minute more before serving.

Ladle the soup into warm bowls. Drizzle over the parsley pesto and scatter the remaining bacon pieces on top.

Rachel's tip
Collect the leek trimmings and parsley stems to add flavour when you are making stock.

Weeknights and everyday

Despite being around food all day, I never tire of cooking, and I cook for my family every day. Like everyone else, I find it useful to have a repertoire of dishes that I know really well and, importantly, that I know my children love eating. These are dishes that are easy to put together but never compromise on flavour. Many of these dishes are one-pot meals, such as the Kale and Bean Stew (page 49) and the Pork and Mushroom Pie (page 77). One-pot meals aren't only easier to cook, they really save on the clearing up!

This chapter includes a recipe for our beloved Irish Stew (page 81). It is a deeply flavoured dish made with lamb or mutton, and each county and even each family has its own version.

Kale and bean stew

Vegetarian (if using vegetable stock)

Serves 6–8

Preparation time: 20 minutes

Cooking time: 40 minutes

3 tbsp extra virgin olive oil

1 carrot, chopped

1 celery stalk, trimmed and chopped

4 shallots, chopped

2 cloves garlic, finely chopped

Salt and freshly ground black pepper

250ml (9fl oz) dry white wine

2 x 400g (14oz) cans white beans, such as cannellini, butter or haricot, drained and rinsed

800ml–1 litre (29fl oz–1¾ pints) Chicken Stock (page 35) or Vegetable Stock (page 34)

3 sprigs of thyme

1 bay leaf

500g (1lb 2oz) shredded kale leaves (stems and centre ribs discarded)

1 tbsp sherry vinegar

2 tbsp fresh parsley, chopped, to serve

I love the deep nourishment that a bean and vegetable stew can provide in winter. Stews such as this warm and hearty one are perfect after a bracing walk in the wind and rain. Kale grows well in Ireland, and it is one of my favourite vegetables. There are a few different varieties. Curly kale is the most popular, but there is also red Russian kale and the fabulous Italian variety known as Tuscan kale, cavolo nero or sometimes dinosaur kale due to its unusual bobbled appearance.

Heat the olive oil in a large saucepan over medium heat. Add the carrot, celery, shallots and garlic. Season with salt and pepper and cook, stirring occasionally, for 10–12 minutes, until completely soft and lightly browned.

Add the white wine, bring to a simmer, and cook for about 5 minutes, or until the liquid is slightly reduced. Add the beans, 800ml (29fl oz) of the stock, the thyme and bay leaf. Bring to a boil, reduce the heat to low, and simmer for about 15 minutes, until slightly reduced.

Add the kale and allow the stew to simmer for 3–5 minutes, until the kale is tender. Remove the thyme and bay leaf. If you would like a thinner stew, add a little more stock at this stage. Stir in the sherry vinegar, then taste for seasoning and serve in bowls with a sprinkling of parsley.

Salad with beetroot, toasted hazelnuts and Cashel Blue dressing

Vegetarian

Serves 4

Preparation time: 10 minutes

Cooking time: 30–45 minutes

4 small beetroot (about 150g/5oz in total)

40g (1½oz) hazelnuts, toasted and roughly chopped

4 handfuls of salad leaves

Finely grated zest of ½ lemon

About 20 slices Cucumber Pickle (page 133) (optional)

FOR THE DRESSING

125ml (4fl oz) extra virgin olive oil

1 tbsp freshly squeezed lemon juice

½ tsp honey

75g (3oz) roughly crumbled Cashel Blue cheese

Salt and freshly ground black pepper

Small, sweet summer beetroot make for a perfect simple salad. Their earthy sweetness works well when balanced with the creamy, salty taste of Cashel Blue cheese. This salad has a much-needed crunch from toasted hazelnuts. If you desire, serve it with Cucumber Pickle (page 133).

First cook the beetroot. Wash the roots carefully under a cold tap. Do not scrub them – simply rub off any dirt with your fingers. You don't want to damage the skin or to cut off the tops or tails, otherwise the beetroot will 'bleed' while cooking. Put the beetroot in a saucepan, cover with cold water and bring to a simmer over medium heat. Cover and continue to simmer for 30–45 minutes, depending on the size and age of your beetroot. They are cooked when their skins rub off easily, and a knife can be inserted easily into the centres. Peel the beetroot by rubbing off and discarding the skins. Then cut each beetroot into eight wedges.

To make the dressing, mix together the olive oil, lemon juice and honey in a bowl or jar, then add the blue cheese and taste, adding salt and pepper as needed.

Combine the beetroot and hazelnuts in a bowl, drizzle with three-quarters of the dressing, season and toss.

Place the salad leaves on one big serving plate or divide among individual plates and drizzle with the remaining dressing. Scatter the beetroot and the hazelnuts over the leaves. Sprinkle over the grated lemon zest. If you desire, you can add four or five slices of cucumber pickle per person.

Leinster

Food in Ireland is characterised by a lavish abundance of natural, earthy produce. A cornucopia of nature's bounty is found in the fields and hedgerows of the counties of Leinster, a region where blue-grey mountains and romantic glens blend seamlessly with fertile lush valleys and majestic woodlands.

In the wild, blackberries, strawberries, sloes, damsons, crab apples, elderflowers, wood sorrel, hairy-leafed comfrey, spicy horseradish and wild nettles are there for the picking. The acidic soils of the Wicklow uplands are the ideal place to find a small, purple fruit that grows on the prickly bilberry shrub. We call these bilberries fraughans. The last Sunday in July heralds the Irish tradition of Domhnach na bhFraocháin, or Fraughan Sunday – the day these tasty berries, cousins of the cranberry, are at their ripest and ready to be gleaned. In times past, Irish families would climb the mountain ridges and fill their baskets with rotund fraughans. Their pickings were exported by boat and train to England, and this provided impoverished families with enough money to pay the grocery bill. Fraughans can be dried for use as 'hedgerow currants', used in jams and jellies, or simply whipped off the bush, simmered in water and sugar, and then folded into some freshly whipped Irish cream to make the toothsome treat of fresh fraughan fool.

Dublin is the home of Guinness, and the famous stout is made inside St. James' Gate using malting barley grown in fields throughout Ireland. Until a decade ago, the addition of Kilkenny-grown hops created the bitterness so characteristic of this Irish dry stout. Today, the craft brewing industry has flourished, and independent microbreweries, such as the Carlow Brewing Company and Kildare's Trouble Brewing, offer an artisanal alternative to Guinness and the like. The annual St. Patrick Day's parade in Dublin isn't the same without a slice of spicy porter cake (see the recipe on page 198), a traditional fruit cake made all the more delicious with the addition of dark, smoky porter and served with a generous dollop of fresh Irish ice cream.

From the medieval fishing village of Slade, near Wexford's Hook Head, to Louth's Carlingford Lough, the chilly Irish Sea air blows across the length of Leinster's coastline. It's little wonder that coastal communities have long celebrated the sea's bounty. In August, the annual Carlingford Oyster Festival honours this salty fresh mollusc. It's a nod to Carlingford's Viking past when the fearless Nordic warriors feasted on this marine delicacy (see page 24 for ways in which you can enjoy this delicacy too). Fish for tea on Friday is a tradition still practised in Ireland, and while salmon and sea trout remain kingly in the eyes of the Irish, delectable oily mackerel and luscious salted herrings (known as kippers) make frequent appearances on our plates.

Wild meat has somewhat faded from our collective consciousness, but there has been a recent resurgence of interest in it, and dishes such as wood pigeon pie, rabbit stew, roasted wild duck and pheasant casserole can be enjoyed in many Irish eateries. Wild deer have long roamed the mountains of Leinster; remains of a medieval deer trap were recently discovered atop Carlow's Blackstairs Mountains, known in Irish as Na Staighrí Dubha. The prolific fallow deer population in Wicklow's Glencree Valley owes its presence to Anglo-Norman lords who introduced them into Ireland in the 12th century. Today, venison makes for a rich, sumptuous addition to traditional Irish stew. If you are more adventurous, try thinly sliced smoked venison, or juicy, iron-rich venison sausages, which are sold in Dublin's famous Temple Bar market each Saturday.

Fish cakes

Serves 4

Preparation time: 10 minutes

Cooking time: 25 minutes

600g (1lb 5oz) floury potatoes

Salt and freshly ground black
pepper

400g (14oz) skinned white fish,
such as cod, haddock or hake

150g (5oz) butter, diced

4 tbsp white wine

Juice of ¼ lemon

150g (5oz) button mushrooms,
sliced

200g (7oz) cooked and peeled
shrimp or small prawns (chop
large ones)

2 egg yolks

1 tbsp Dijon mustard

4 tbsp finely chopped fresh herbs,
such as parsley, tarragon, dill
or chives (either one herb or
a mixture)

3–4 tbsp extra virgin olive oil

Salad leaves and lemon wedges,
to serve

This is a particularly good fish cake recipe, great for using up leftovers, but I rarely make the same fish cakes twice. I use whatever fish I can get and vary the other ingredients, too. Sometimes I like to add chillies, or use different cooked vegetables or different herbs. In summer we love to eat these outside with a tomato and basil salad and some flavoured mayonnaise (see the flavoured mayonnaise that accompanies the Dublin Bay Prawns on page 16). In winter I prefer them with an herb butter melting over the top.

Scrub the potatoes, but do not peel them. Place in a large saucepan, cover with cold water, and add a good pinch of salt. Bring the water to a boil and cook the potatoes for 10 minutes. Then pour out all but about 3cm (1in) of the water and continue to cook the potatoes over very low heat. Don't be tempted to stick a knife into them at any stage to see if they are cooked – the skins will split and the potatoes will just break up and become soggy if you do. About 20 minutes later, when you think the potatoes might be cooked, test them with a skewer; if they are soft, take them off the heat and drain them.

Peel the potatoes while they are still hot, holding them in a clean tea towel to avoid scalding your hands. Mash them immediately and transfer to a large bowl.

Meanwhile, place the fish in a wide, shallow saucepan and add 100g (3½oz) of the butter, the wine and the lemon juice. Season with salt and pepper, then cover with a lid and gently poach over low heat for 10–15 minutes, until the fish is cooked through. Carefully remove the fish from the pan and set aside to cool a little. Turn up the heat to high and boil the poaching liquid until it has reduced by half.

In the meantime, melt 25g (1oz) of the remaining butter in a small frying pan over medium heat. Add the mushrooms and sauté for 8–10 minutes, until soft and golden, seasoning with salt and pepper. Set aside and allow to cool a little.

Add the fish, reduced poaching liquid and cooked mushrooms to the mashed potatoes along with the shrimp, egg yolks, mustard and herbs. Gently mix everything together, breaking the fish up as you go but being careful not to mash it up too much. Season to taste with salt and pepper.

recipe continues overleaf

Shape the mixture into eight patties, each about 8cm (3in) wide and 2cm (¾in) thick, and arrange on a baking tray or large plate. Cover with cling film and place in the fridge for about 1 hour to firm up. (The fish cakes can be prepared up to this stage in advance and either frozen or kept in the fridge for up to 24 hours.)

Combine the olive oil and remaining butter in a large frying pan over medium–low heat and very gently fry the fish cakes for about 5 minutes on each side, or until golden and warmed through, adding a little more oil or butter to the pan during cooking if necessary.

Divide the fish cakes among the serving plates, add some salad leaves to each plate, and serve immediately with lemon wedges and flavoured mayonnaise (page 16) or Herb Butters (below).

Herb butters

Vegetarian

Each recipe **Makes** about 85g (3½oz)

Preparation time: 5 minutes

FOR THE DILL BUTTER

75g (3oz) butter, softened

1 heaped tbsp finely chopped fresh dill

Squeeze of lemon juice

Salt and freshly ground black pepper

FOR THE GARLIC AND HERB BUTTER

75g (3oz) butter

3 cloves garlic, crushed

1 heaped tbsp finely chopped mixed fresh herbs

Salt and freshly ground black pepper

Herb butter is easy to make, using whatever herbs are on hand. To store, spoon it onto some greaseproof paper, roll into a sausage shape, securing the ends, and pop in the fridge or freezer. Slice the butter as you need it.

Dill butter
Mash the butter with a fork in a small bowl to soften. Stir in the dill, along with a good squeeze of lemon juice and a little salt and pepper. Store in the fridge or freezer until ready to use.

Garlic and herb butter
Mash the butter with a fork in a small bowl to soften. Stir in the garlic, herbs and a little salt and pepper. Store in the fridge or freezer until ready to use.

Fish stew

Serves 4–6

Preparation time: 15 minutes

Cooking time: 20 minutes

450g (1lb) mussels

4 large tomatoes

4 tbsp olive oil

200g (7oz) leeks, trimmed and cut into 7mm (⅜in) thick slices

1 red pepper, deseeded and cut into 1–2cm (½–¾in) dice

Salt and freshly ground black pepper

300ml (11fl oz) Chicken Stock (page 35) or fish stock

Good pinch of caster or granulated sugar

12 raw, peeled king prawns, langoustines or tiger prawns (about 225g/8oz in total)

300g (11oz) skinless white fish fillets, such as cod or haddock, cut into 2cm (¾in) chunks

2 tbsp chopped fresh parsley, to serve

This is a lovely light fish stew that just cries out for crusty bread to mop up all the delicious juices. Use whatever seafood is at its freshest – a combination of contrasting tastes and textures is what you're aiming for. Serve with Brown Soda Bread (page 227) or Ballymaloe Brown Yeast Bread (page 230).

First prepare the mussels. Rinse the shells in cold running water a couple of times to wash away any sand or grit. Give them a scrub to dislodge any barnacles or bits of weed, then remove the 'beard' with a tug or a sharp knife. Discard any that are open and won't close when tapped against a hard surface.

Peel the tomatoes by scoring a cross at the top of each tomato with a sharp knife, then placing in a bowl and covering with boiling water. Leave in the water for 15–20 seconds, then drain, rinse in cold water and peel the skin from each tomato. Chop the peeled tomatoes into small pieces and set aside.

Pour the olive oil into a large saucepan on medium heat, add the leeks and red pepper and season with salt and pepper. Cook for 4 minutes or until a little softened, then add the chopped tomatoes, stock and sugar. Bring to a boil, then reduce the heat, cover with a lid, and cook for 7–8 minutes more or until the tomatoes are soft.

Tip in the mussels, prawns and fish, bring back up to a boil, then reduce the heat, cover with the lid and simmer gently for 2–3 minutes or until the fish and seafood are cooked. (The fish and prawns should be opaque and the mussels opened – discard any that remain closed.)

Season to taste, sprinkle over the parsley and serve with chunks of crusty bread.

Fish pie

Serves 4–6

Preparation time: 15 minutes

Cooking time: 1 hour 10 minutes

1 large onion, peeled and chopped

800g (1¾lb) skinless fish fillets, either one type or a mixture, such as salmon, cod, whiting, hake or haddock

150ml (5fl oz) white wine

Juice of ½ lemon

125g (4½oz) butter, diced

Salt and freshly ground black pepper

150g (5oz) mushrooms, sliced

225ml (8fl oz) double or whipping cream

1 heaped tbsp Dijon mustard

4 tbsp finely chopped mixed fresh herbs, such as chives, parsley, tarragon, thyme or dill

Creamy Mashed Potato (page 166)

This is the fish pie that my husband Isaac makes, and it's a wonderful family supper. The rich creamy fish filling is offset by the lemon juice and Dijon mustard. This fish pie can be made in advance, not cooked, and kept in the freezer for up to three months.

Preheat the oven to 180°C/350°F/Gas Mark 4.

Put the onion in the bottom of a large saucepan and lay the fish on top in an even layer (cutting to fit, if necessary). Pour in the wine, add the lemon juice (the liquid is unlikely to cover the fish, but that's fine), scatter three-quarters of the butter over the top and season with salt and pepper. Cover with a lid and simmer over low heat for 15–20 minutes, until the fish is cooked.

In the meantime, melt the remaining butter in a small frying pan over low heat and sauté the mushrooms for 5–6 minutes, until softened. Season well with salt and pepper.

Using a slotted spoon, carefully transfer the fish from the saucepan (leaving the onions and cooking liquid in the pan) to a 22cm (8in) square ovenproof dish or divide among four to six individual gratin dishes. While there is no need to flake the fish, you needn't worry if the fish breaks up as you move it.

Add the cream to the onions and cooking liquid in the pan and continue to simmer, with the lid off, for 10–15 minutes, until the sauce is reduced and thick enough to coat the back of a spoon. Stir in the mustard, herbs and sautéed mushrooms and check the seasoning.

Pour the sauce over the fish in the dish (or dishes) and then spoon over the mashed potato, spreading with the back of a spoon or fork. Alternatively, pipe the mashed potato over the fish with a pastry bag and nozzle for a more professional-looking finish. (The fish pie can be prepared to this stage, left to cool, and then placed in the fridge overnight until you are ready to bake, if wished.)

Bake in the oven for about 30 minutes, or until bubbling and golden on top. Add about 10 minutes if the pie has been chilled. Serve immediately.

Chicken casserole with cheesy herb dumplings

Serves 6–8

Preparation time: 30 minutes

Cooking time: 1 hour 10 minutes

1 whole chicken (1.8kg/4lb)

Salt and freshly ground black pepper

2 tbsp olive oil

350g (12oz) thick-cut or unsliced bacon, cut into 1–2cm (½–¾in) chunks

1 large onion, roughly chopped

2 large carrots, sliced 2cm (¾in) thick on the diagonal

700ml (1¼ pints) Chicken Stock (page 35) or Vegetable Stock (page 34)

Few sprigs of thyme

FOR THE CHEESY HERB DUMPLINGS

350g (12oz) plain flour, plus extra for dusting

1 tsp bicarbonate of soda

1 tsp salt

2 tbsp finely chopped mixed fresh herbs, such as parsley, thyme, rosemary, tarragon or chives

300ml (11fl oz) buttermilk or soured milk (see tip on page 228)

4 tbsp finely grated Cheddar cheese

This is such a perfect family meal: a steaming pot for the centre of the table, just the kind of food I want on a blustery day. It's really easy to make and the dumplings are a fantastic alternative to potatoes or bread. I like to serve this dish with a green salad.

Preheat the oven to 180°C/350°F/Gas Mark 4.

Remove the breasts from the chicken and cut them in half. Remove the leg portions and divide them into thighs and drumsticks. This will make eight chicken pieces in total. Season them well with salt and pepper.

Pour the olive oil into a large flameproof casserole dish over high heat, add the bacon and fry for 1–2 minutes, until crisp. Remove with a slotted spoon and drain on kitchen paper. Add the chicken in batches and sear on each side until golden, then remove. Add the onion and carrots and fry for 2–3 minutes, until golden.

Return the bacon and chicken to the casserole dish, pour in the stock, add the thyme and season with salt and pepper. Bring slowly to a boil, cover with a tight-fitting lid and bake in the oven for 20 minutes.

In the meantime, prepare the dumplings. Sift the flour, bicarbonate of soda and salt into a large bowl and stir in the herbs. Make a well in the centre and pour in most of the buttermilk (leaving about 50ml/2fl oz in the measuring jug). Using one hand with your fingers outstretched like a claw, bring the flour and liquid together, adding a little more buttermilk if necessary. Don't knead the mixture or it will become too heavy. The dough should be soft but not too wet and sticky.

Tip the dough onto a floured work surface and bring together, forming it into a round. Using a rolling pin, roll the dough out to a thickness of about 2cm (¾in). With a 5cm (2in) biscuit cutter, stamp out 10–12 dumplings, or divide the dough into 10–12 pieces and roll each one between your hands into a small ball.

Remove the casserole dish from the oven and turn the heat up to 230°C/450°F/Gas Mark 8. Arrange the dumplings on top, leaving slight gaps to allow for spreading. Sprinkle with the cheese. Return to the oven, uncovered, for 10 minutes. Reduce the heat to 200°C/400°F/Gas Mark 6 and bake for another 20 minutes, or until the dumplings are crisp and golden and the chicken is cooked through.

Turkey and ham potato pie

Serves 6–8

Preparation time: 10 minutes

Cooking time: 1 hour

50g (2oz) butter

1 onion, finely chopped

450g (1lb) mushrooms, sliced

350ml (12fl oz) double cream

100ml (3½fl oz) turkey or Chicken Stock (page 35)

675g (1½lb) mixed leftover cooked turkey and ham, cut into 1cm (½in) chunks

1 tbsp chopped fresh tarragon or marjoram

Salt and freshly ground black pepper

Creamy Mashed Potato (page 166)

This is a pie we tend to make after Christmas Day, when we have both leftover turkey and ham. We also call it St. Stephen's Day Pie, and it's always incredibly popular in our house, even with the disappointment of Christmas being over! You can use chicken or another bird if you don't have leftover turkey. Try serving with Buttered Leeks (page 147) or Creamed Kale (page 147).

Preheat the oven to 180°C/350°F/Gas Mark 4.

Melt half of the butter in a large saucepan over low heat. Add the onion and fry gently for 8–10 minutes, until completely soft but not browned. Remove from the pan and set aside. Increase the heat and add the remaining butter to the pan. Tip the mushrooms into the pan and sauté for 4–5 minutes, until they are soft and golden brown (you may need to do this in two batches).

Return the onion to the pan and pour in the cream and stock. Bring to a boil, then reduce the heat and simmer for 3–4 minutes, until the sauce has thickened a little. Add the turkey, ham and tarragon and season to taste with salt and pepper. Pour into a shallow 3 litre (5 pint) gratin dish set on a baking tray and spread evenly. Top with the mashed potato, spooning it on in dollops and spreading with a fork.

Bake for 25–30 minutes in the oven, until golden brown on top and bubbling hot.

Rachel's tip
Rather than making one large pie, divide the ingredients among six to eight individual pie dishes. This is also particularly handy if you choose to freeze them (fully made with the mashed potato on top). Then you can take them out as you need them.

Homemade pork sausages with colcannon and apple sauce

Serves 4 (makes about 12 sausages)

Preparation time: 15 minutes

Cooking time: 40 minutes

450g (1lb) fatty minced pork

50g (2oz) fresh breadcrumbs

1 egg, lightly beaten

1 clove garlic, crushed

1 tbsp chopped fresh parsley or marjoram

Salt and freshly ground black pepper

3 tbsp olive oil or sunflower oil

FOR THE COLCANNON

1.5kg (3lb) floury potatoes, scrubbed

100g (3½oz) butter

500g (1lb 2oz) green cabbage, outer leaves removed

2 tbsp water

250ml (9fl oz) milk, heated

2 tbsp chopped fresh parsley

Salt and freshly ground black pepper

FOR THE APPLE SAUCE

1 large cooking apple (350g/12oz), peeled, cored and roughly chopped

1 tbsp water

25–50g (1–2oz) caster sugar

For me there is nothing quite so comforting as bangers and mash, and these homemade sausages are ever so tasty and easy to make. Colcannon is perfect winter food.

To make the sausages, mix together the pork, breadcrumbs, egg, garlic and parsley. Season with salt and pepper. Fry a tiny bit of the mixture in a pan with a little olive or sunflower oil to see if the seasoning is good.

Divide the mixture into twelve portions and shape each one into a sausage. Place on a baking tray or plate and set aside until you want to cook them. (Chilling them for a day in the fridge is fine, or you can freeze them.)

To make the colcannon, cook the potatoes, covered, in boiling salted water for 10 minutes. Then drain three-quarters of the water and continue to cook over low heat with the lid on for another 20–30 minutes until cooked. Test using a skewer or feel with your fingers; avoid stabbing the potatoes with a knife because this will make them break up. When cooked, drain all the remaining water, peel and mash with 50g (2oz) of the butter while hot. I usually hold the potato on a fork and peel with a knife if they are hot.

Meanwhile, cook the cabbage. Cut the cabbage into quarters, then cut out the core. Thinly slice the cabbage across the grain. Heat a saucepan, add the remaining butter, water and the sliced cabbage. Toss over medium heat for 5–7 minutes, until just cooked. Add to the potatoes, then add most of the hot milk and the parsley, keeping some of the milk back in case you do not need it all.

Season to taste and beat until creamy and smooth, adding more milk if necessary.

While the potatoes are cooking, make the apple sauce and cook the sausages. To make the apple sauce, put the apple in a small saucepan with the water. Cover and cook over gentle heat (stir every now and then) until the apple has broken down to a mush. Add sugar to taste.

To cook the sausages, heat a frying pan over low–medium heat, add 2 tablespoons of the olive oil and gently fry the sausages for 12–15 minutes, until golden on all sides and cooked on the inside. Serve with the colcannon and apple sauce.

Dublin coddle

Serves 4–6

Preparation time: 5 minutes

Cooking time: 30 minutes

350g (12oz) potato, peeled and cut into 2cm (¾in) cubes (more or less)

200g (7oz) finely chopped onion

225g (8oz) breakfast sausages, each cut into 4 pieces

600ml (1 pint) leftover bacon cooking liquid, Chicken Stock (page 35) or water

Salt and freshly ground black pepper

100g (3½oz) leftover boiled or fried bacon, torn or cut into 1–2cm (½–¾in) chunks (more or less)

1 tbsp finely chopped fresh parsley

Coddle is a simple Irish dish long associated with Dublin and spoken of in rapturous tones by many of us from the city. It is a mixture of potato, bacon, onion and sausage all cooked in a flavourful broth. This is a recipe from my husband Isaac, which he made one Monday using leftover bacon and the cooking water from the previous evening's boiled bacon (see page 112). The use of the cooking water gives this coddle recipe real depth of flavour, but it's incredibly simple to put together. If you don't have leftover boiled bacon, you can make this dish using fried rashers or lardons of bacon and chicken stock or even water.

Put the potato, onion and sausages in a large saucepan and add the bacon cooking water. Add a little salt and pepper (but not too much if you're using bacon cooking water). Place over medium heat and bring to a boil, then simmer for about 30 minutes, until the potatoes are just tender. Add the cooked bacon and cook for another few minutes. Stir in the parsley, season to taste and serve immediately.

Ham and egg pie

Serves 6–8

Preparation time: 20 minutes

Cooking time: 40 minutes

Shortcrust Pastry (page 72)

15g (½oz) butter

1 onion, chopped

6 eggs

75ml (3fl oz) double cream

150g (5oz) cooked ham or bacon, sliced into 1 x 2cm (½ x ¾in) pieces

1 tbsp chopped fresh parsley

Salt and freshly ground black pepper

This is a lovely, old-fashioned picnic pie. You can serve it for lunch, but it travels well for a picnic. This is the sort of thing people used to make to bring to work with them; in fact, you could do the same! If you have any left over, it makes a handsome breakfast. Try serving with Tomato Relish (page 20) and a green salad.

Preheat the oven to 180°C/350°F/Gas Mark 4.

Roll out the pastry and line a 25cm (10in) pie dish. Trim the pastry so that it is a bit bigger than the dish, then fold up the edges slightly so that you have a little lip all the way around. This will prevent the cream from running out when you put the pie in the oven. Refrigerate while you prepare the filling.

For the filling, melt the butter in a small saucepan over low heat, add the onions and cook until soft, 5–8 minutes. Whisk two of the eggs in a bowl, add the cream, the cooked onions, chopped ham and parsley. Season with salt and pepper. Pour this into the pastry case. Carefully break the remaining eggs onto the pie, trying to keep the egg yolks intact.

Bake for 25–35 minutes, until the custard is set in the centre and the eggs on top are just cooked. Serve warm or allow to cool and pack for a picnic. Cut slices of the pie straight from the dish.

Shortcrust pastry

Vegetarian

Makes 450g (1lb)

Preparation time: 55 minutes
(including cooling)

Cooking time: 17–22 minutes

250g (9oz) plain flour

125g (4½oz) butter, diced and
softened

½–1 egg, beaten

This makes enough to line one (28cm/11in) square or one (25cm/10in) round tin (with a little left over) or two (20cm/8in) square tins (it is best if they have removable bases). Uncooked pastry freezes perfectly, so it is handy to have some in the freezer. It will also keep in the fridge for a couple of days.

Combine the flour and butter in a food processor. Whiz for a few seconds, then add half the beaten egg and continue whizzing. You might need to add a little more egg, but don't add too much – the pastry should just come together. (If making by hand, rub the butter into the flour, then use your hands to bring it together with the egg.) Flatten out the ball of dough to a thickness of about 3cm (1¼in), wrap or cover with cling film, and chill for at least 30 minutes.

When you are ready to roll the pastry, remove from the fridge. Place the pastry between two sheets of cling film, which should be bigger than your tart tin. Using a rolling pin, roll it out until it is no thicker than 3mm (⅛in). Make sure to keep it round, if the tin is round, and large enough to line the bottom and sides of the tin.

Remove the top layer of cling film and place the pastry upside-down (cling film side facing up) in the tart tin. Press into the edges, cling film still attached and, using your thumbnail, cut the pastry on the edge of the tin to give a neat finish. Remove the cling film and pop the pastry in the freezer for at least 10 minutes.

Blind baking

Blind baking is a way of partially cooking a pastry case before adding its filling. Preheat the oven to 180°C/350°F/Gas Mark 4. Line the pastry with greaseproof paper when cold (leaving plenty to come up the sides), fill with ceramic baking beans or dried beans (you can use these over and over) and bake for 15–20 minutes, until the pastry feels dry. Remove the paper and beans, brush with a little leftover beaten egg and return to the oven for 2 minutes. Take out of the oven and put to one side while you prepare the filling. This can be made a day in advance.

Variation

Sweet pastry: Use the recipe for shortcrust pastry above, but add 25g (1oz) icing sugar to the flour and butter in the food processor at the start of the recipe.

Pork chops with sage and apple

Serves 4

Preparation time: 10 minutes

Cooking time: 15 minutes

25g (1oz) butter

2 tbsp extra virgin olive oil

4 pork loin chops (each about 1.5cm/¾in thick)

Salt and freshly ground black pepper

2 apples, peeled and cut into 5mm (¼in) slices

200ml (7fl oz) cider

4 tbsp crème fraîche or sour cream

4 tsp chopped fresh sage

Sage and apple are the autumnal flavours of Ireland. Sweet apples are the perfect partner for pork. Smooth apple sauce, of course, goes well with roast pork, but here there are apple slices, which retain their bite. I think it's especially fitting that this recipe then uses cider to finish everything off. If you can, use our delicious dry Irish cider. You could serve this with Sautéed Potatoes with Caramelised Onions (page 162), Roast Garlic Colcannon (page 170), Root Vegetable Mash (page 165) or Buttered Cabbage (page 144).

Combine the butter and olive oil in a large frying pan over high heat. When the butter starts to foam, place the chops in the pan and season with salt and pepper. Cook on one side for 2–3 minutes, until golden underneath, then turn over and season again.

Add the apple slices to the pan, nestling them in among the pork. Cook for about 5 minutes, tossing the slices regularly, until the apples are golden and softened and the chops are cooked through.

Pour in the cider and stir in the crème fraîche and sage. Bring to a simmer and allow to bubble for a couple of minutes, or until slightly thickened. Season with salt and pepper to taste and serve.

Pork and mushroom pie with gentle spices

Serves 4

Preparation time: 15 minutes

Cooking time: 1¾ hours

25g (1oz) butter

2 onions, chopped

Salt and freshly ground pepper

1 tsp ground cumin

1 tsp ground coriander

680g (1½lb) pork (shoulder or leg, fat removed), cut into 1–2cm (½–¾in) cubes

250ml (9fl oz) Chicken Stock (page 35)

1 tbsp extra virgin olive oil

300g (11oz) button mushrooms, sliced, left whole or quartered

250ml (9fl oz) single cream

1 tbsp chopped fresh parsley

FOR THE ROUX

25g (1oz) butter

20g (¾oz) plain flour

FOR THE TOPPING

300g (11oz) puff or shortcrust (flaky) pastry, rolled 5mm (¼in) thick

1 egg, beaten

OR

Creamy Mashed Potato (page 166)

Cumin and coriander seem to be the two spices I reach for the most and run out of most often, they both go well with pork. The filling for the pie can be made a day in advance and left in the fridge, giving the spices time to infuse the meat. Then cover with mashed potato or buttery pastry.

Preheat the oven to 160°C/325°F/Gas Mark 3.

To make the filling, melt the butter in a medium-size flameproof casserole dish, add the onions and season with salt and pepper. Cover and sweat over low heat for 5 minutes. Turn up the heat and add the cumin, coriander and pork. Toss for a few minutes until the pork changes colour, then add the stock. Cover and bake in the oven for 45–60 minutes, until the pork is tender.

While the pork is cooking, heat the olive oil in a pan over high heat and toss in the mushrooms. Cook for a few minutes until they are pale golden. Add to the pork after it has baked for 30 minutes.

When the pork is tender, remove the pork and mushrooms from their cooking liquid and set aside in a dish in a warm place. Add the cream to the juices in the casserole dish and boil with the lid off for a few minutes until the flavour intensifies.

To thicken the sauce, first make the roux. Melt the butter in a medium-size saucepan over medium heat. Add the flour, stirring, and allow it to cook for 2 minutes then remove from the heat. Slowly stir the roux into the boiling cooking liquid. Add the chopped parsley and return the pork and mushrooms. Season to taste and spoon into individual gratin dishes or a large pie dish.

For a pastry topping, preheat the oven to 230°C/450°F/Gas Mark 8. For a mashed potato topping, preheat it to 180°C/350°F/Gas Mark 4.

For a pastry top, cut the pastry to the same size as the top of the pie dish and arrange over the filling. Make a hole in the centre for steam to escape. Brush with the beaten egg to glaze. Bake for 10 minutes, then turn down the oven temperature to 190°C/375°F/Gas Mark 5 and bake for about 20 minutes, until the pastry is golden brown.

For a mashed potato top, arrange the mashed potato on top of the filling and lightly score the surface. Bake for 30–40 minutes, until golden brown on top and bubbling hot.

Lamb chops with parsley and mint sauce

Serves 4–6

Preparation time: 5 minutes

Cooking time: 10 minutes

8–12 lamb loin chops

4 tbsp extra virgin olive oil

Salt and freshly ground black
pepper

FOR THE PARSLEY AND MINT SAUCE

Handful of mint leaves

2 handfuls of parsley leaves

2 tbsp capers, drained and rinsed

8 tinned anchovies

6 tbsp extra virgin olive oil

2–4 tbsp freshly squeezed lemon
juice

Salt and freshly ground black
pepper

A parsley and mint sauce is an easy way of adding flavour to lamb chops. The anchovies give the sauce a wonderful depth that works particularly well with lamb and doesn't taste at all fishy. The mint and parsley bring freshness while the capers give the sauce their own particular punchy flavour. You can make the sauce ahead and it will keep in a jar for up to two weeks in the fridge. Do take it out of the fridge about half an hour or so before serving, to give the flavours a chance to wake up.

The sauce would also be an excellent accompaniment to grilled steak, roast chicken or pan-fried mackerel. You could also serve with Pea and Spring Onion Champ (page 169).

To make the sauce, combine the herbs, capers, anchovies, olive oil and 2 tablespoons of the lemon juice in a food processor. Whiz for a minute, then add salt and pepper or more lemon juice to taste. If you don't have a food processor you can chop everything finely by hand and mix together.

Place a frying pan or griddle pan over high heat. While it is heating, drizzle the lamb chops with the olive oil and season with salt and pepper. Place in the hot pan and cook for 2–4 minutes on each side, until just pink in the centre. Serve immediately with a drizzling of the sauce.

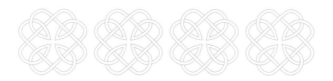

Irish stew

Serves 4–6

Preparation time: 10 minutes

Cooking time: 1½–2 hours

1.5kg (3lb 4oz) mutton or lamb chops from the neck or shoulder, still on the bone, cut about 1.5cm (¾in) thick

3 tbsp extra virgin olive oil

3 carrots, cut into thick slices at an angle, or 12 small baby carrots, scrubbed and left whole

12 baby onions, or 3–4 medium onions, cut into quarters through the root, which should keep the wedges intact

Salt and freshly ground black pepper

400ml (14fl oz) lamb stock, Chicken Stock (page 35) or water

8–12 potatoes, peeled, and halved if very large

1 sprig of thyme

1 tbsp chopped fresh parsley

1 tbsp snipped fresh chives

The definitive recipe for Irish stew simply doesn't exist because each household has its own family recipe. It is said, however, that people in the south of Ireland always add carrots, but people north of County Tipperary do not. Many people make their stew by placing alternate layers of meat, onions, carrots and potatoes, seasoned with salt and pepper, in a pot, covering with water, and stewing gently for a couple of hours. If you sear the meat and vegetables before stewing, as we do at Ballymaloe, it seals in the delicious sweet flavours.

Preheat the oven to 160°C/325°F/Gas Mark 3.

Cut the chops in half, but keep the bones intact as they will give great flavour. Heat the olive oil in a medium to large flameproof casserole dish. Toss in the meat and cook for a minute on both sides, until nice and brown. Remove the meat and set aside. Add the carrots and onions to the hot oil and cook for a couple of minutes, seasoning with salt and pepper. Return the meat to the casserole dish. Add the stock and bring to a boil. Put the potatoes in, season again with salt and pepper and place a sprig of thyme on top.

Cover and bake in the oven for 1½–2 hours, until the meat is very tender. When it is cooked, pour off the cooking liquid and allow it to sit for a minute until the fat floats to the top; adding a cube of ice will help speed this up. Spoon off the fat and pour the juices back over the stew. Add the chopped herbs and serve.

Rachel's tip

If the potatoes are quite small, add them 20–30 minutes after the stew starts cooking to avoid them breaking up.

Special family dinners

For me there are few things more gratifying than cooking a special dinner for my whole family. Often it's a particular family member's favourite, such as Isaac's Hot Buttered Lobster (page 90), the Pot-roasted Duck Legs (page 106) that my son Joshua loves so much, or a roast chicken (page 96) that the whole family adores. Making fabulous meals should never be reserved just for serving guests. Your family is just as deserving, if not more deserving, of such treats!

These are great recipes but they're never fussy. They're big, warming, convivial dishes that are perfect for sharing. There are some real Irish classics in here, such as Boiled Bacon and Cabbage (page 112) and Beef and Red Wine Hot Pot (page 130), a hearty supper beloved of everyone whose mother made it for them.

You'll also find lots of fantastic fish recipes in this chapter. Being an island, Ireland offers a wonderful selection of fresh fish wherever you live in the country. I think the best way of serving such great fish is to not do too much with it and serve it quite simply, with perhaps a Herb Butter (page 56) or Hollandaise Sauce (page 12).

Salmon with capers and dill

Serves 4

Preparation time: 5 minutes

Cooking time: 10 minutes

50g (2oz) butter, diced

4 (125g/4½oz) salmon fillets (with the skin left on, if you wish)

Salt and freshly ground black pepper

4 tbsp capers, drained and rinsed

2 tbsp freshly squeezed lemon juice mixed with 6–8 tbsp water

4 tsp chopped fresh dill

I always have a jar of capers in my fridge – they're a great shortcut to a good punchy flavour. Here, they cut through the rich oily fish. This dish can be made in just a few minutes, and I like to serve it simply with some boiled new potatoes. Instead of salmon, it would be just as good with fresh mackerel, an equally oily fish. The fish goes particularly well with Pea and Spring Onion Champ (page 169).

Place a frying pan over medium–high heat. When it is hot, add a couple of knobs of butter, very quickly followed by the salmon, skin side down. Fry for 3–4 minutes, until golden brown underneath. Turn over, season with salt and pepper and fry for another couple of minutes, or until the fish is just cooked through. (The timing will depend on the thickness of the salmon fillets and heat of the pan.)

Add the capers, along with the remaining butter and lemon juice mixture and boil for 1 minute. Season to taste, adding more lemon juice or water, if necessary. Transfer the salmon onto warmed plates, stir the chopped dill into the sauce and pour over the fish to serve.

Pan-fried mackerel with herb butter

Serves 4

Preparation time: 5 minutes

Cooking time: 5 minutes

8 mackerel fillets, with the skins on

75g (3oz) plain flour, seasoned with salt and pepper

25g (1oz) butter, softened

Lemon wedges, to serve

FOR THE HERB BUTTER

100g (3½oz) butter, softened

2 tbsp chopped fresh herbs

1 tbsp freshly squeezed lemon juice

My son Joshua will often fish for mackerel off the pier in late summer when the mackerel are at their best. He and his friends will bring back a few delicious fish, which he loves to cook himself. It is said the sun should never set on a mackerel; certainly it is a fish that must be eaten as fresh as possible. This is a simple but absolutely divine way to serve one of my favourite fish. Serve with Creamy Mashed Potato (page 166) and a green salad or Pea Purée (page 150) if you desire.

To make the herb butter, cream the butter in a bowl and add the chopped herbs and the lemon juice. Roll into a sausage shape and wrap in greaseproof paper or cling film. Put into the freezer to chill quickly.

Place a frying pan or a griddle pan over high heat and wait for it to get very hot. When the pan is hot, dip the fillets in the seasoned flour and shake off the excess. Spread the flesh side (not the skin side) with a little soft butter and place butter side down on the hot pan. Cook for a couple of minutes, until crisp and golden, then turn over and cook the other side for another 2–3 minutes, turning down the heat if the pan is getting too hot.

Serve on hot plates with one or two slices of herb butter slowly melting on the fish, with a wedge of lemon on the side.

Trout baked in parchment paper

Serves 4

Preparation time: 5 minutes

Cooking time: 15 minutes

40g (1½oz) butter, softened

2 tbsp chopped fresh parsley

1 tbsp chopped fresh thyme

1 tbsp chopped fresh dill

Salt and freshly ground black pepper

4 trout fillets (or salmon or mullet), about 125g (4½oz) each

Trout in all their different colours have always been eaten in Ireland. There are lakes and rivers all over the country full of this delicious and delicately flavoured fish. Trout is available in fishmongers or, of course, you can catch it yourself!

By cooking fish in a parcel of baking parchment, all the flavours from the fish and this herb butter are sealed in. It also ensures the fish is kept perfectly moist. I love serving this dish to guests and watching each person open their own parcel and breathe in the gorgeous aromas from the herbs and fish.

Try serving with Creamy Mashed Potato (page 166) and Minted Broad Beans (page 150) or Pea Purée (page 150).

Preheat the oven to 220°C/425°F/Gas Mark 7.

For each serving, cut out a piece of parchment paper or foil measuring about 30cm (12in) square.

To make the herb butter, mix together the butter, parsley, thyme and dill in a bowl and season with salt and pepper.

Place a piece of fish in the centre of the paper and add a spoonful (a quarter) of the herb butter. Fold the square in half to enclose he filling and then fold in the edges to seal and form a parcel. The finished parcel should be semi-circular in shape, looking rather like a Cornish pasty. Repeat for the other pieces of fish and place on a baking tray.

Bake for 12–14 minutes, until the fish is just opaque all the way through. You'll need to open one to check; this can be yours. Place the parcels on serving plates for people to open for themselves.

Rachel's tip
You could also make this dish with whole trout, though they will take longer to cook, about 25–30 minutes.

Hot buttered lobster

Serves 4

Preparation time: 30 minutes

Cooking time: 30 minutes

2 (900g/2lb) live lobsters

Salt and freshly ground black pepper

1 carrot, sliced

1 onion, sliced

2 celery stalks, sliced

600ml (1 pint) water

600ml (1 pint) dry white wine

2 sprigs of parsley

2 sprigs of thyme

1 bay leaf

A few peppercorns

50g (2oz) butter

Juice of 1 lemon, plus wedges to garnish

I think this is the best way of serving lobster – it's simply about presenting that wonderfully sweet meat of the most impressive of shellfish. I adore lobster straight from the sea. This decadent dish is strictly for special occasions. It's important that when you're cooking the steamed lobster in the butter you allow the butter to get quite golden as that really intensifies the sweet flavour. Serve with nothing more than boiled new potatoes.

A couple of hours before you are ready to cook, put the lobsters in a plastic bag in the freezer. When it is time to cook them, bring a large saucepan of salted water (3 tablespoons salt to every 2 litres/3½ pints water) to a boil.

Plunge the frozen lobsters directly into the boiling water and when they start to turn colour from dark to browny orange, in about 10 minutes, remove them from the pan and discard the water.

Put the carrot, onion, celery, water, wine, herbs and peppercorns into the same saucepan and bring to a boil. Add the lobsters and cover with the lid. Cook until they turn a very bright orange-red: for a 900g (2lb) lobster this will be about 20 minutes and for a 1.3kg (3lb) lobster this will be about 30 minutes. When they are cooked, take them out of the pan and let them cool. Strain the cooking liquid and use as fish stock (it will freeze).

Once the lobsters are cool enough to handle, turn the lobster over so the softer belly is facing upwards. With a large, sharp knife cut them in half lengthways from head to the tail as evenly as possible. Extract all the meat from the head and from the tail and claws. You will need to use either a wooden mallet or the flat edge of a chopping knife blade to crack open the claws. Chop the meat into 2cm (¾in) chunks.

Clean the lobster shells (keeping the head and tail intact, if possible, to serve the lobster in) and pop into a low oven along with your plates just to heat up.

Melt the butter in a frying pan over high heat. When it's hot and foaming, add the lobster meat and toss for about a minute. Season with lemon juice and pepper. Using a slotted spoon, divide the lobster among the half shells on warmed plates then spoon the juices over the lobster meat. Serve immediately with wedges of lemon and see your guests melt in ecstasy!

 Ulster

In the long history of Irish food, the humble spud is relatively new to our plate. The early Irish didn't know this vegetable; a typical meal for them would have been bread and milk, perhaps flavoured with salted meat, cabbage, onion and seaweed. It is the potato, however, with which we are so closely identified. Traditional to northwest Ireland is a dish known as boxty, or 'poor-house bread' (see the recipe on page 168). It dates back to early 19th-century pre-famine times when the watery 'lumper' potato was abundant. Potatoes at the bottom of the barrel, perhaps past their best, were used to make poor-house bread. The potato was grated and mashed, then drained in a cotton pillow case that was hung from the door. The yellowish liquid was collected in a bowl below and used as a source of starch for washing clothes. The drained potatoes were mixed with flour and a grain of salt, then cooked on a cast-iron griddle over an open fire. A slice of boxty topped with a fried egg makes for a warm, filling winter's breakfast.

Armagh is in Orchard County. For more than 3,000 years, apple trees have grown in these fertile, loam soils. The orchards are bound by tall hedgerows that act as windbreakers to protect the young apple crop. In autumn, Armagh apple growers keep a close eye on the size and sweetness of their Bramley apples; the skin must be solid green with a reddish flush, the flesh a white colour with a hint of green. October's harvest is celebrated with a traditional apple festival, and local people enjoy eating these tangy, firm apples in a variety of dishes: Armagh Bramley apple pie and Bramley apple soup are served with a glass of Armagh cider.

The home of the potato in Ulster is Comber, where the land is sheltered by the Mourne Mountains and the Ards Peninsula and protected from the sharp frosts by Strangford Lough. This micro-climate warms the soil. Comber potatoes are ready to lift in May, and locals anticipate early summer with a flurry of excitement and joy as these unique potatoes are ready to eat. The nutty, distinctive flavour is best tasted when these potatoes are seasoned and served with a round of fresh Irish butter. Many believe that champ – a traditional dish of mashed potatoes blended with spring onions, butter, salt and pepper (see the recipe on page 169) – is only authentic when made with Comber potatoes. By European law, Comber spuds are so unique that, like Champagne, their status is protected.

The unpolluted waters off Donegal and the north coast are replete with wild seafoods. For generations, coastal communities have gleaned carrageenan moss, winged kelp, razor clams, dillisk, periwinkles, cockles, oysters, mussels and more. Home-smoking was a strong tradition in Ireland as a way to deal with a glut of fresh fish caught in the sea. Fish were rubbed with sea salt and stored in a cold shed near the house. During the lean winter months the dried fish would be sliced and enjoyed with boiled potatoes, cabbage and Irish butter.

A special prize is reserved for the one hundred and fifty fishing families who live in the five provinces that touch the shores of Ireland's biggest lake, Lough Neagh, because it is in these waters that Europe's largest commercial wild eel fishery is found. The fishermen's cooperative operates a strictly controlled fishery to ensure the prospects of future generations of eel fishermen. Public houses such as the oldest thatched pub in Northern Ireland, the Crosskeys Inn, serve this salty, fatty fish to local people as a way to celebrate the end of the eel fishing season in October.

Steamed mussels with cream and herbs

Serves 4

Preparation time: 10 minutes

Cooking time: 10 minutes

2.5kg (5½lb) mussels

150ml (5fl oz) double or whipping cream

1 tbsp chopped fresh parsley

1 tbsp chopped fresh chives

2 tsp chopped fresh thyme

2 tsp chopped fresh fennel (the herb, not the bulb)

Everyone in our family adores mussels, and this dish is a convivial social food, with a great big bowl of steaming mussels in the centre of the table and crusty bread to share. The novelty of removing each mussel from its shell can be very enticing for young and old alike. In this recipe you can use a mixture of your favourite fresh herbs or whatever you have on hand. Tarragon, chervil, dill and marjoram all work perfectly, in addition to the ones suggested here. There is no need to season this dish because the juices from the mussels will probably be salty enough. Serve with Brown Soda Bread (page 227) or Ballymaloe Brown Yeast Bread (page 230).

Scrub the mussels very well, discarding any that are open and don't close when tapped against a hard surface. Remove the beard – the little fibrous tuft – from each mussel.

Pour the cream into a large saucepan and bring slowly to a boil. Stir in the herbs and add the mussels. Reduce the heat to a simmer, cover with a lid and continue to cook over medium heat for 5–8 minutes, until all the mussels are completely open. (Discard any that remain closed.)

Scoop the mussels out into one large or four individual serving bowls and ladle the creamy juices over. Place another bowl on the table for the empty shells, some finger bowls and lots of napkins.

Roast chicken with stuffing and gravy

Serves 4–6

Preparation time: 5 minutes

Cooking time: 1½–1¾ hours

Traditional Herb Stuffing (or one of the variations) (page 161)

1 whole chicken (1.5–2.25kg/3⅓–5lb)

15g (½oz) butter, softened

Salt and freshly ground black pepper

Chicken Gravy (page 98) or Tarragon Cream Sauce (page 99)

I'm often asked what dish most brings me back to my childhood, and it is without a doubt roast chicken. In the winter we always stuff the bird. In the summer, though, I often forgo the stuffing for something a little lighter – just a few cloves of garlic and a lemon.

Of course, roast chicken is fantastic with a simple gravy, but why not experiment with a cream sauce, such as the Tarragon Cream Sauce on page 99 – most definitely Isaac's favourite!

Serve with Granny's Roasted Herbed Potatoes (page 158), Sticky Cumin and Apricot Roast Carrots and Parsnips (page 155), Buttered Cabbage (page 144) and Root Vegetable Mash (page 165).

First make the stuffing (if using). Allow to cool.

Preheat the oven to 180°C/350°F/Gas Mark 4.

Spoon the cooled stuffing into the chicken cavity and place the chicken in a roasting tin. Smear the butter over the skin and sprinkle with salt and pepper. Roast for 1½–1¾ hours (allowing about 20 minutes per 450g/1lb), basting occasionally, until cooked through. If the skin begins to look quite dark during cooking, cover the chicken with some foil or greaseproof paper.

To check whether the chicken is fully cooked, stick a skewer into the thigh with a spoon placed underneath to catch the juices; the juices should run clear. Also, the legs should feel quite loose on the bird. When cooked, transfer the chicken to a serving plate and leave to rest, covered with foil and in the oven at the lowest temperature, if possible, while you make the gravy or sauce using the juices of the cooked chicken.

To serve, spoon the stuffing out of the chicken into a serving bowl or onto a plate. Carve the chicken and serve with the stuffing and gravy or any other accompanying sauce.

Rachel's tip
Always buy as good a chicken as you can afford, remembering not only that this is going to be great on the day you cook it, but also that you can then use the leftovers in a soup, pie or pasta sauce, and even make a stock out of the carcass.

Chicken gravy

Makes about 400ml (14fl oz)

Preparation time: 5 minutes

Cooking time: 5 minutes

600ml (1 pint) Chicken Stock (page 35)

25g (1oz) butter

20g (¾oz) plain flour

Salt and freshly ground black pepper

Gravy is, of course, the classic accompaniment to roast chicken. You can use the same method for making gravy for any roast meat.

Once the chicken is cooked and removed from the roasting tin to rest and keep warm (see page 96), place the tin over medium heat and deglaze with a little of the stock, stirring with a wooden spoon and scraping any sticky bits from the bottom of the tin.

Drain off the fat using a separating jug or, if you don't have one, pour the liquid into a bowl and add a handful of ice cubes. After a few minutes, the fat will float to the surface. Remove and discard the fat; pour the remaining liquid into a saucepan with the remaining chicken stock over medium heat.

To make a roux, melt the butter in a medium-size saucepan over medium heat. Add the flour, stirring, and allow it to cook for 2 minutes, then remove from the heat.

Bring the stock and tin juices to a boil, whisk in the roux a little at a time and continue to boil for 2–3 minutes to thicken very slightly. Season to taste with salt and pepper. Just before serving the chicken, strain the gravy through a fine sieve into a gravy boat or jug.

Tarragon cream sauce

Makes about 250ml (9fl oz)

Preparation time: 5 minutes

Cooking time: 5 minutes

600ml (1 pint) Chicken Stock (page 35)

100ml (3½fl oz) double or whipping cream

2 tbsp chopped fresh tarragon

25g (1oz) butter (optional)

20g (¾oz) plain flour (optional)

This is particularly good with roast chicken made with the Smoked Bacon Stuffing (page 161). The recipe assumes you have just roasted a chicken.

Once the chicken is cooked and removed from the roasting tin to rest and keep warm (see page 96), place the tin over medium heat and deglaze with a little of the stock, stirring with a wooden spoon and scraping any sticky bits from the bottom of the tin.

Drain off the fat using a separating jug or, if you don't have one, pour the tin juice into a bowl and add a handful of ice cubes. After a few minutes, the fat will float to the surface. Remove and discard the fat; pour the remaining tin juices into a saucepan with the remaining chicken stock.

Bring the stock and juices to a boil over medium heat and add the cream and tarragon. Simmer for 3–4 minutes, uncovered, stirring regularly, until reduced and thickened. If you'd like it even thicker you can use a roux. To make the roux, melt the butter in a medium-size saucepan over medium heat. Add the flour, stirring, and allow it to cook for 2 minutes, then remove from the heat. Whisk the roux into the tarragon sauce, a little at a time, over low heat.

Chicken open-pot roast

Serves 4

Preparation time: 10 minutes

Cooking time: 35–40 minutes

3 tbsp extra virgin olive oil

1 chicken, cut into pieces, or
4 chicken thighs or breasts
(with the skin left on)

Salt and freshly ground black
pepper

450g (1lb) new potatoes (unpeeled),
larger ones halved

2 small leeks or 1 large leek,
trimmed and cut into
3cm (1in) lengths

250ml (9fl oz) Chicken Stock
(page 35)

1 sprig of tarragon, plus 1 tbsp
chopped fresh tarragon

4 tbsp freshly squeezed lemon juice

1 tbsp Dijon mustard

It's at the end of May that the first of the new season's potatoes begin to appear. We adore spuds, and each year brings such excitement because there is just nothing quite like a freshly dug new potato, be it from a local farm or, even better, from your own garden.

This dish is my light and summery take on chicken casserole. Cooked in an open pot, the chicken skin is allowed to get golden and crisp, but there is still plenty of delicious sauce, which the new potatoes readily soak up. Serve with a green salad.

Preheat the oven to 220°C/425°F/Gas Mark 7.

Pour the olive oil into a large, wide flameproof casserole dish over high heat. Season the chicken pieces with salt and pepper and place, skin side down, in the hot oil. Cook for 4–5 minutes, until a deep golden brown. Turn over, so that the skin side is now on top. Add the potatoes and leeks, season with salt and pepper, and gently stir for another 2 minutes, being careful to keep the chicken skin side up. Pour in the stock and add the sprig of tarragon. Bring to a boil.

Transfer to the oven, uncovered, and bake for about 30 minutes, or until the potatoes are tender and the chicken is cooked through. Remove from the oven, stir in the chopped tarragon along with the lemon juice and mustard and serve immediately.

Roast duck with potato stuffing

Serves 4

Preparation time: 10 minutes

Cooking time: 2 hours

1 whole duck (about 1.8kg/4lb)

Salt and freshly ground black
  pepper

FOR THE STUFFING

15g (½oz) butter

½ onion (about 125g/4½oz),
  chopped

125g (4½oz) peeled and chopped
  cooking apple

1 large floury potato (225g/8oz),
  unpeeled

1 tsp finely grated orange zest

2 tsp chopped fresh thyme leaves

Salt and freshly ground black
  pepper

FOR THE GRAVY

300ml (11fl oz) Chicken Stock
  (page 35) or duck stock

25g (1oz) butter

20g (¾oz) plain flour

*Duck is a bird rich with flavour and a divine coating of glorious fat.
Cooking duck means taking advantage of that wonderful fat and
a potato stuffing is perfect. The mashed potato and apple soaks up
all those delicious juices, just as stuffing should!*

*A golden, crisp-skinned duck makes a magnificent centrepiece. Serve
with Granny's Roasted Herbed Potatoes (page 158), Sticky Cumin and
Apricot Roast Carrots and Parsnips (page 155) and Buttered Cabbage
(page 144).*

First make the stuffing. Melt the butter in a saucepan over medium
heat. When the butter foams, add the onion and apple. Reduce the
heat to low, cover and sweat for 7–10 minutes, until soft. Remove
from the heat.

While the onions and apples are cooking, start cooking the potato.
Put the potato in a large saucepan of cold water with a good pinch of
salt. Bring to a boil and cook for 10 minutes, then pour all but about
4cm (1½in) of the water out of the pan and continue to cook the
potato over very low heat. (Don't be tempted to stick a knife into it
because the skin will break, and the potato will just disintegrate and
get soggy if you do.)

About 20 minutes later, when you think the potato might be cooked,
test with a skewer; if the potato is soft, take it off the heat. Peel the
potato while still hot and mash immediately; add to the apple and
onion mixture. Stir in the orange zest and thyme and season with
salt and pepper. Allow to get quite cool before stuffing your duck.

Preheat the oven to 180°C/350°F/Gas Mark 4.

Season the cavity of the duck with salt and pepper and spoon in the
stuffing. Place the duck on a rack in a roasting tin and pierce the skin
all over with the point of a sharp knife (this will help release the fat
during cooking). Season the skin well, particularly with salt, to help
crisp it up during cooking.

Roast for about 1½ hours, allowing about 20 minutes per 450g/1lb,
basting occasionally and draining any excess fat from the tin. When
the duck is cooked, the legs should feel slightly loose and a metal
skewer inserted into the thigh should be too hot to hold against

recipe continues overleaf

the inside of your wrist. When cooked, transfer the duck to a serving plate and leave to rest, covered with foil, in the oven at the lowest temperature, if possible, while you make the gravy.

Drain any fat from the roasting tin using a separating jug or, if you don't have one, pour the liquid from the tin into a bowl and add a handful of ice cubes. After a few minutes the fat will float to the surface. Remove and discard the fat (saving it, if you wish, for roast potatoes on another day), then pour the remaining cooking juices into a saucepan.

To make the gravy, first make a roux. Melt the butter in a medium-size saucepan over medium heat. Add the flour, stirring, and allow it to cook for 2 minutes, then remove from the heat. Set aside. Place the roasting tin over medium heat and deglaze with a little of the cooking juices or stock, stirring with a wooden spoon and scraping any sticky bits from the bottom of the tin. Pour this into the saucepan with the cooking juices, add the remaining stock and bring to a boil. Whisk in the roux, a little at a time, and continue to boil for 2–3 minutes to thicken to the desired consistency. Season to taste with salt and pepper if necessary. Just before serving, strain the gravy through a fine sieve into a warm gravy boat or jug.

Spoon the stuffing out of the duck into a serving bowl or onto a serving plate. Carve the duck breasts away from the carcass and cut each one in half. Remove the leg portions and divide them in half, too. Serve a breast and leg portion to each person, along with some stuffing and gravy.

Pot-roasted duck legs with onions and root vegetables

Serves 4

Preparation time: 10 minutes

Cooking time: 1–1½ hours

1½ tsp extra virgin olive oil

4 duck legs, excess fat removed, but with the skin left on

4 onions, halved through the root, each half cut lengthways into 4 wedges

4 sprigs of rosemary

Salt and freshly ground black pepper

6 floury potatoes, peeled and cut into 2cm (¾in) dice

6 small white turnips, peeled and cut into 1–2cm (½–¾in) dice

This is the food I love to serve on a wintery weekend evening when friends are over. It's a dish for an easy-going dinner party, to serve with plenty of red wine and lots of laughter.

There are large sweet turnips, but I prefer the small white ones because they're more refined in flavour and are particularly at home with duck or goose.

Preheat the oven to 200°C/400°F/Gas Mark 6.

Heat the olive oil in a flameproof casserole dish over medium heat. Add the duck legs, skin side down, followed by the onions, rosemary and salt and pepper. Cook for 4–5 minutes, until the skin is a rich golden brown. Tip in the potatoes and turnips and cover with a lid.

Roast in the oven for 1–1¼ hours, by which time the onions should be golden and the root vegetables and duck cooked through and tender.

Irish weekend fry-up

Serves 1

Preparation time: 10 minutes

Cooking time: 25 minutes

Vegetable, sunflower or olive oil, for frying

Butter, for frying and spreading on toast

1–2 medium-size pork sausages

1–2 rashers thick-cut, dry-cured, smoked or unsmoked, back or streaky bacon, rind removed

2–3 slices of black and/or white pudding

50g (2oz) button mushrooms, sliced, or 1 large flat mushroom, stem removed

Salt and freshly ground black pepper

1 ripe tomato, halved

Pinch of caster sugar (if roasting the tomato in the oven)

FOR THE EGGS

1–2 eggs

½ tbsp milk (for scrambled eggs)

15–20g (½–¾oz) butter (for scrambled eggs)

2 slices white or brown bread

A fry-up is great when friends are staying over – simply multiply the ingredients given below by however many people you are feeding. Source the best local ingredients you can and follow up with a big walk. You can have your eggs boiled or poached, if you prefer.

Our family eats an Irish breakfast or some parts of it at least once a week, and not always in the morning. We're lucky to have great producers of bacon and, of course, black and white pudding, which is a particular speciality of Cork County. Black pudding (blood sausage) may be more popular worldwide, but white pudding is very popular in Ireland and an important part of an Irish breakfast. White pudding is similar to black pudding, but it contains no blood – only pork, spices and usually oatmeal. I love this big cooked breakfast, but it isn't something I'll eat early in the morning before I go for a run!

Heat 1 tablespoon oil and 1 tablespoon butter in a large frying pan over medium heat. Add the sausages and fry for 10–15 minutes, until golden and cooked through. Add the bacon and fry for 3–4 minutes on each side, until crisp and golden, dabbing off any milky liquid with kitchen paper. Add the black and/or white pudding slices to the pan and fry for 2–3 minutes on each side, until beginning to crisp; the white pudding (if using) should turn golden. Remove the sausages, bacon and pudding slices from the pan and drain on kitchen paper.

Place in an ovenproof dish in a low oven to keep warm.

Meanwhile, add a dash of oil and knob of butter to another frying pan over medium heat. Add the button mushrooms and sauté for 3–4 minutes, until softened and turning golden. Season with salt and pepper, then remove from the pan and keep warm (adding to the dish with the sausages and bacon). If you are cooking a large flat mushroom, then add the oil and butter to the pan and fry the mushroom for 8–10 minutes, turning halfway through, until softened and browned.

Season the cut side of the tomato halves with salt and pepper and drizzle over 1 tablespoon of oil. Gently fry them, cut side down first, for 2–3 minutes, then turn over and fry for another 2–3 minutes, until just softened.

recipe continues overleaf

Alternatively, cook the large flat mushroom and/or the tomatoes in the oven. Preheat the oven to 200°C/400°F/Gas Mark 6. Drizzle 2 teaspoons of olive oil over or add a knob of butter to the mushroom and season with salt and pepper before roasting for 12–15 minutes until tender. Put a knob of butter on the cut side of each tomato half, add the sugar and season with a little salt and pepper before roasting for 12–15 minutes, until softened. If you are using the oven, begin roasting the mushroom and tomatoes a few minutes before frying the sausages and bacon. Once cooked, reduce the oven temperature to low for keeping everything warm as it is cooked.

To fry an egg, melt a knob of butter in a small, clean frying pan over low heat. Carefully crack the egg into the pan and allow to fry gently. For an over-easy egg, fry for 1–2 minutes, until it begins to set, then flip over and fry for another 1–2 minutes. If you prefer your egg sunny side up, then fry gently for 4–5 minutes, until the yolk has filmed over. Remove from the pan and serve immediately with the other cooked ingredients.

For scrambled eggs, crack the eggs into a bowl, add the milk, season with salt and pepper and beat together. Add 1 tablespoon of the butter to a small saucepan over low heat. Immediately pour in the eggs and cook for 2–3 minutes, stirring continuously (I find a wooden spatula best for this), until the butter has melted and the eggs are softly scrambled. Remove from the heat immediately so that the eggs don't become overcooked. Serve with the other cooked ingredients.

While the egg is cooking, put the slices of bread in a toaster or toast under a preheated grill for a few minutes (and on both sides, if using the grill) until golden. Butter the toast and cut the slices in half.

To serve, arrange everything on a warm serving plate, with the hot buttered toast on the side and with some tomato ketchup (see opposite) or relish.

Rachel's ketchup

Vegetarian

Makes about 200ml (7fl oz)

Preparation time: 10 minutes

Cooking time: 1 hour 10 minutes

2 tbsp extra virgin olive oil

225g (8oz) onions, roughly chopped

650g (1½lb) roughly chopped
   tomatoes (about 6 small to
   medium tomatoes)

2 cloves garlic, crushed or finely
   grated

75ml (3fl oz) white wine vinegar

75g (3oz) caster or granulated sugar

2 tsp Dijon mustard

Pinch of ground allspice

Pinch of ground cloves

½ tsp salt

½ tsp freshly ground black pepper

If your children regularly eat ketchup, then you might want them to try this delicious and much healthier homemade version. If you think they won't take to it, ease them into it by mixing some into their usual brand and gradually adjusting their taste. This is definitely best made in the summer with lovely ripe red tomatoes. It keeps for many weeks in the fridge because of the vinegar and sugar. It's possible to freeze the sauce – perhaps as ice cubes for speedy thawing.

Heat the olive oil in a saucepan over medium heat. Add the onions and sauté for 8–10 minutes, until softened and a little golden. Add the tomatoes, garlic, white wine vinegar, sugar, mustard, allspice, cloves, salt and pepper. Cover with a lid and simmer for about 30 minutes, or until very soft.

Remove from the heat and purée in a food processor or using a hand-held blender. Pour through a sieve into a clean saucepan and simmer, uncovered and stirring regularly, for another 30 minutes, or until the mixture is thick.

Pour into sterilised jars (see page 188) and store in the fridge.

Bacon and cabbage with parsley sauce

Serves 6

Preparation time: 20 minutes

Cooking time: 1½ hours

900g (2lb) piece back bacon or cured and smoked pork loin (loin or collar of bacon)

1 small savoy cabbage, outer leaves removed

25g (1oz) butter

Salt and freshly ground black pepper

FOR THE PARSLEY SAUCE

300ml (11fl oz) Basic White Sauce (page 114)

1 tsp Dijon mustard

25g (1oz) finely chopped fresh parsley

Salt and freshly ground black pepper

This is a traditional Irish dish in which the cabbage is boiled in the water used for cooking the bacon. Many people recall it with affection, while others remember it for the overcooked cabbage. Providing the cabbage is cooked for only 3–5 minutes, you won't be disappointed. This dish is also delicious served with Creamy Mashed Potato (see page 166), or boiled or baked potatoes and some hot mustard.

Put the bacon in a large saucepan, cover with water and bring slowly to a boil. Drain, refill the pan with fresh water, and repeat. This is to get rid of the salt (which appears as white froth on top of the water), so it may need to be done again, depending how salty the bacon is. Taste the water to check for saltiness and keep checking and boiling again in fresh water until you are happy with the flavour.

Cover with fresh hot water and bring to a boil for the final time. Reduce the heat, cover with a lid, and simmer for about 40 minutes (allowing 20 minutes per 450g/1lb), occasionally skimming any sediment that rises to the surface. Once the bacon is cooked (a skewer inserted in the middle should come out easily), remove from the pan (reserving the cooking liquid) and let rest, covered with foil, a clean tea towel or upturned bowl.

In the meantime, prepare the parsley sauce. Make the white sauce following the instructions on page 114, then stir in the mustard and parsley. Check the seasoning and adjust if necessary. Cover and keep warm in the pan.

Cut the cabbage into quarters, remove the core and finely shred across the grain. Bring the cooking liquid for the bacon to a fast boil. Add the cabbage and cook for about 3 minutes, until just tender (it's easy to overcook). Drain well, squeezing out any excess water, and return to the saucepan. Add the butter to the cabbage, tossing to melt, and season to taste with salt and pepper.

Remove and discard the rind from the bacon, if necessary, and slice the bacon into thick pieces. Serve the bacon with the buttered cabbage and parsley sauce.

Basic white sauce

Vegetarian

Makes about 300ml (11fl oz)

Preparation time: 5 minutes

Cooking time: 20 minutes

300ml (11fl oz) whole milk

Few slices of carrot

Few slices of onion

1 sprig of parsley

1 sprig of thyme

3 peppercorns

15g (½oz) plain flour

15g (½oz) butter

Salt and freshly ground black pepper

This makes a sauce thick enough to coat the back of a spoon. It is thickened using a roux, which is made from flour and butter cooked together. If you would like a thicker sauce, use twice as much butter and flour when making your roux.

Pour the milk into a small saucepan and add the carrot, onion, parsley, thyme and peppercorns. Bring to a boil, reduce the heat, and simmer for 4–5 minutes. Remove from the heat and leave to infuse for about 10 minutes.

While the milk infuses, make the roux. Melt the butter in a small saucepan over low–medium heat and add the flour. Allow to cook for 2 minutes, stirring regularly. Set aside.

Strain the milk through a sieve placed over a small saucepan and bring the milk to a boil. Whisk in the roux, a little at a time, until well blended and allow to simmer gently for 4–5 minutes, or until thickened to the desired consistency. Season to taste and use as a plain white sauce or add your choice of flavouring.

Rachel's tip

For a speedier version, melt the butter in a large saucepan on medium heat and add the flour, stirring for a few seconds. Take off the heat and gradually add the milk, stirring continuously until the milk is fully incorporated and the sauce is lump free. Return the pan to gentle heat and cook the sauce for 6–8 minutes, stirring constantly, until thickened and smooth.

Crumbed bacon chops with sweet whiskey sauce

Serves 4–6

Preparation time: 10 minutes

Cooking time: 1¼ hours

900g (2lb) piece back bacon, unsmoked

110g (3½oz) plain flour

1 egg

110g (3½oz) fresh white breadcrumbs

Salt and freshly ground black pepper

25g (1oz) butter

1 tbsp extra virgin olive oil

FOR THE WHISKEY SAUCE

225g (8oz) sugar

75ml (3fl oz) cold water

50ml (2fl oz) hot water

3–4 tbsp Irish whiskey

This is a dish often made at Ballymaloe. I adore the crispy coating around the bacon chops and the way the sweetness of the sauce combines perfectly with the saltiness of the bacon. Serve with some vegetables and boiled new potatoes or Creamy Mashed Potatoes (page 166). If you're feeding children, leave the whiskey out of the sauce because the alcohol does not burn off. Substitute orange or pineapple juice.

Put the bacon in a large saucepan, cover with water and bring slowly to a boil. Drain, refill the pan with fresh water and repeat. This is to get rid of the salt (which appears as white froth on top of the water), so it may need to be done again, depending how salty the bacon is. Taste the water to check for saltiness and keep checking and boiling again in fresh water until you are happy with the flavour.

Cover with fresh hot water and bring to a boil for the final time. Reduce the heat, cover with a lid, and simmer for about 40 minutes (allowing 20 minutes per 450g/1lb), occasionally skimming any sediment that rises to the surface. Once the bacon is cooked (a skewer inserted in the middle should come out easily), lift out of the water, drain well and allow to cool a little.

Meanwhile, prepare the sauce. Put the sugar in a saucepan with the cold water and bring slowly to a boil over low heat, stirring until the sugar dissolves. Boil without stirring for about 10 minutes, until it turns a chestnut-brown colour, swirling the pan to caramelise evenly. Remove from the heat and immediately add the hot water. Stir to make a smooth sauce, then add the whiskey. Keep warm in the pan.

Sift the flour into a wide shallow bowl, beat the egg in a small bowl, put the breadcrumbs in a third dish and season all three with salt and pepper. Remove the bacon rind (if not already removed), and slice into chops 1–2cm (½–¾in) thick. Dip each chop first in the flour, then in the egg and finally in the breadcrumbs to coat.

Combine the butter and oil in a large frying pan over medium heat. When the butter starts to froth, fry the chops for 3–4 minutes on each side, until crisp and golden. Serve the crumbed bacon chops with the sweet whiskey sauce drizzled over.

Kinoith pork casserole

Serves 6–8

Preparation time: 20 minutes

Cooking time: 2 hours

1.5kg (3lb 4oz) bone-in shoulder pork chops, cut about 1cm (½in) thick

3 tbsp extra virgin olive oil

Salt and freshly ground black pepper

12 baby onions, peeled (see tip), or 3–4 standard onions, cut into quarters lengthways through the root

3 carrots, thickly sliced, or 12 baby carrots, scrubbed and left whole

8cm (3in) piece of fresh ginger, peeled and finely grated

1 litre (1¾ pints) Chicken Stock (page 35)

1.3kg (3lb) potatoes (about 12 small), peeled, and halved if large

3 tbsp chopped fresh coriander

My father-in-law Timmy created this recipe, and we eat it regularly. The ginger flavour is quite subtle, so feel free to increase the amount, if you wish. If you use loin chops, there is probably no need to remove any fat after cooking.

Preheat the oven to 170°C/325°F/Gas Mark 3.

Cut the pork chops in half without removing the bones because they will greatly add to the flavour. Heat the olive oil in a flameproof casserole dish with a tight-fitting lid over high heat. When the oil is really hot, add the meat in batches, searing the chops for about 1 minute on each side, or until golden brown, seasoning with salt and pepper as it cooks. Remove from the dish and set aside.

Add the onions and carrots to the hot oil and sauté for 3–4 minutes, until soft; season with salt and pepper. Return the chops to the dish. Add the ginger, pour in the stock and bring to a boil. Put the potatoes on top of the chops, cover with a lid and bake for 1½–1¾ hours, until the meat is very tender and the sauce has thickened slightly.

Once cooked, strain the stew through a colander over a large bowl to catch the cooking liquid. Return the meat and vegetables to the dish with the lid on to keep warm and let the liquid stand for a minute or so to allow the fat to float to the top (adding some ice cubes will help speed up the cooling process). Remove the fat with a spoon and return the liquid to the dish. Warm through over low heat, stir in the coriander and serve.

Rachel's tips

You can replace the olive oil with 3 tablespoons of fat rendered from the pork. Heat any pork fat trimmings from the meat in a small saucepan until melted to a liquid.

If the potatoes are quite small, add them to the dish 20–30 minutes after the stew starts cooking to prevent them from breaking up.

To quickly peel the baby onions, place them in a bowl, cover with boiling water and allow to stand for a few minutes before draining. The skins should then peel off very easily.

Slow-roasted shoulder of pork

Serves 6–8

Preparation time: 15 minutes

Cooking time: 6 hours 20 minutes

3–4kg (6–8lb) bone-in pork shoulder

Salt and freshly ground black pepper

1 bulb garlic, broken up into cloves (unpeeled)

1 butternut squash (about 900g/2lb) with skin, deseeded and cut into 1–2cm (½–¾in) cubes

4 trimmed leeks (about 375g/13oz) in total), cut into 1cm (½in) thick slices

Small handful of sage leaves

I love that with this gorgeous dish you simply put the pork in the oven in the morning, then carry on with your day. By dinnertime you'll have the most succulent and tender piece of meat. The shoulder is one of the cheaper cuts of pork and, when cooked correctly, it is definitely my favourite. It demands to be cooked slowly, allowing the fat to melt and moisten the meat and giving the flavours time to develop. When this pork is ready, it is so tender you don't need to carve it into slices, and nor would you be able to. Just pull off succulent shreds of the meat and pieces of crispy crackling and serve with the roasted vegetables.

Preheat the oven to 220°C/425°F/Gas Mark 7.

Using a sharp knife, score the rind of the pork in a crisscross pattern at 5mm (¼in) intervals, cutting through the fat but not into the meat itself (or ask your butcher to do this for you, if you prefer). Sprinkle over 1 tablespoon of salt, rubbing it into the lines scored in the fat, place the pork in a large roasting tin and roast in the oven for 30 minutes. Reduce the temperature to 150°C/300°F/Gas Mark 2 and continue to cook for another 5 hours.

Remove the pork from the oven and turn the temperature up to 220°C/425°F/Gas Mark 7. Pour off the fat into a bowl, leaving any juices in the tin. Place the garlic, squash, leeks and sage leaves around the pork. Then pour over 3 tablespoons of the reserved fat, season with salt and pepper and toss the vegetables together in the tin. Return to the oven for 40–50 minutes, until the pork rind has turned into delicious crackling, and the vegetables are cooked through and golden. Serve from the tin or transfer to a large plate.

Roast pork belly with a cumin and garlic rub

Serves **4–6**

Preparation time: 10 minutes

Cooking time: 3¾–4¼ hours

About 1.5kg (3lb 4oz) pork belly, rind left on

300ml (11fl oz) Chicken Stock (page 35)

Salt and freshly ground black pepper

FOR THE CUMIN AND GARLIC RUB

2 tbsp cumin seeds, toasted and ground

6 cloves garlic, peeled

2 tsp salt

2–3 tbsp extra virgin olive oil

Pork belly is the perfect expression of pork, with just the right amount of wonderfully flavourful fat, which not only tastes fabulous but also keeps the meat incredibly moist. Belly needs to cook for quite a long time in order for (nearly) all the fat to come out and for the crackling to become deliciously crisp and crunchy. Make sure that the rind is still on when you buy it (it's essential for the crackling!). Serve with Root Vegetable Mash (page 165) and Buttered Cabbage (page 144).

Preheat the oven to 150°C/300°F/Gas Mark 2.

For the rub, combine the cumin, garlic and salt and whiz everything together using a hand-held blender, or just finely chop everything by hand and mix together well in a bowl. Add enough olive oil to form a rough paste.

Score the rind on the pork belly, using a very sharp knife and making long cuts through the rind and into the fat (but not into the meat), from one side of the fat to the other at roughly 5mm (¼in) intervals.

Massage the paste into the scored lines in the rind and place the meat rind side up in a roasting tin. Roast in the oven for 3½–4 hours, until the meat is very tender (you should be able to cut the meat with a spoon). Turn up the heat to 220°C/425°F/Gas Mark 7 and roast for another 10–15 minutes, until the rind is crisp and crackly.

Transfer the pork to a serving plate and allow to rest in the oven, with the heat turned off, or somewhere warm for at least 15 minutes.

While the pork is resting, make the gravy. Pour off any excess fat from the roasting tin, then place the tin over medium heat and deglaze by pouring in the stock, whisking continuously to dissolve the caramelised juices sticking to the bottom of the tin. Pour the juices into a separating jug or pour the liquid into a bowl and skim off the melted fat from the surface. It can help to add a few ice cubes; the fat will solidify and float to the surface after a few minutes, and you can then scoop it out and discard it.

Return the meat juices to a small saucepan, bring to a boil, season with salt and pepper if necessary, then pour into a jug to serve straight away or reheat when you are ready to serve.

Carve the pork into slices and serve with the gravy.

Lamb shanks with potatoes and pearl barley

Serves 4

Preparation time: 10–15 minutes

Cooking time: 3½ hours

2 tbsp extra virgin olive oil

4 lamb shanks

Salt and freshly ground black pepper

4 red onions, cut lengthways through the root end into 6 wedges

4 cloves garlic, finely chopped

4 tomatoes, cut into 3cm (1in) chunks

1 tsp caster sugar

50g (2oz) pearl barley

500ml (18fl oz) Chicken Stock (page 35)

About 1.3kg (3lb) floury potatoes, peeled and quartered

Every August for a few years running, I cooked for a wonderful American couple who owned a house in Ireland. On dull rainy days they would request this most comforting dish. It's very convenient to make because most of the ingredients just go into the pot together and the only thing you have to think about after that is adding the potatoes.

Preheat the oven to 150°C/300°F/Gas Mark 2.

Pour the olive oil into a flameproof casserole dish over medium–high heat. Season the lamb shanks with salt and pepper. When the oil is hot, add the shanks and cook for about 4 minutes on each side, or until they begin to brown. Add the onions, garlic, tomatoes, sugar, pearl barley and chicken stock. Bring to a boil, then cover with a lid and bake in the oven for 2½ hours.

Add the potatoes, cover again and return to the oven for another 50–60 minutes, until the potatoes are cooked and the lamb shanks meltingly tender.

Leg of lamb with roasted vegetables

Serves 6–8

Preparation time: 15 minutes

Cooking time: 1¾–2 hours

1 bone-in leg of lamb
(3–4kg/6½–8¾lb)

Salt and freshly ground black
pepper

750g (1lb 10oz) floury potatoes,
peeled and cut into 7mm (⅜in)
slices

3 parsnips (about 450g/1lb in total),
peeled and cut into 7mm (⅜in)
slices

3 red onions, cut lengthways
through the root end into
1cm (½in) wedges

1 tbsp fresh thyme leaves or
chopped rosemary leaves

3 tbsp extra virgin olive oil

Redcurrant Jelly (page 128) or Mint
Sauce (page 128), to serve

A Sunday roast can sometimes take some time to put together and to coordinate all the side dishes. This recipe avoids that altogether because the lamb is cooked on a rack over the vegetables allowing them to soak up all the juices and flavour of the meat and saving you time cooking and clearing up! When you are buying the leg of lamb, ask your butcher to remove the aitchbone at the top of the leg and trim the knuckle from the end.

Preheat the oven to 180°C/350°F/Gas Mark 4.

If necessary, remove the papery skin from the lamb. Then, using a sharp knife, make long shallow scores in a crisscross pattern in the fat, spacing the lines 3cm (1in) apart, and season well with salt and pepper.

Combine the potatoes, parsnips, onions, thyme and olive oil in a large roasting tin and toss together, seasoning with salt and pepper. Spread everything out in the tin and place the lamb on a rack over the top (if you don't have a rack, place the lamb in the roasting tin and surround it with the vegetables). Roast for 1½ hours, or until the lamb is cooked to your desire.

Remove the tin from the oven and increase the heat to 220°C/425°F/Gas Mark 7. Transfer the lamb to a large plate or a board sitting in a tray, cover with foil and leave to rest somewhere warm.

Put the vegetables back in the oven and roast for another 20–30 minutes, or until golden on top.

About 10 minutes before the vegetables are ready, start carving the lamb. Then divide among plates, adding spoonfuls of the vegetables, and serve with redcurrant jelly or mint sauce.

Redcurrant jelly

Vegetarian

Makes 3 x 300ml (11fl oz) jars

Preparation time: 5 minutes

Cooking time: 10 minutes

500g (1lb 2oz) fresh or frozen (and defrosted) redcurrants, stems removed

500g (1lb 2oz) granulated or caster sugar

Delicious with roast meat, especially lamb (see page 126), this will keep for months in sterilised jars in the fridge. Use frozen redcurrants instead of fresh, if necessary.

Combine the redcurrants and sugar in a large, heavy saucepan and stir over medium heat until the sugar dissolves and the mixture comes to a boil. Increase the heat and boil for 6 minutes, stirring every now and then to prevent it from sticking to the bottom of the pan. Spoon off any froth that has come to the top.

Pour the mixture into a non-reactive sieve. Allow it to drip through without pushing it with a spoon (which will cause the jelly to become cloudy) and then place in clean, sterilised jars (see Rachel's tip on page 188).

Mint sauce

Vegetarian

Makes 75ml (3fl oz)

Preparation time: 10 minutes

3 tbsp chopped fresh mint

1 heaped tbsp granulated or caster sugar

50ml (2fl oz) boiling water

1 tbsp freshly squeezed lemon juice or white wine vinegar

The classic accompaniment to roast lamb (see page 126), mint sauce is best made on the day, up to a couple of hours before serving.

Combine the mint and sugar in a small bowl and pour over the boiling water. Stir to dissolve the sugar, then stir in the lemon juice. Let stand for at least 10 minutes before serving.

Beef and red wine hot pot

Serves 6

Preparation time: 15 minutes

Cooking time: 2½ hours

3–4 tbsp extra virgin olive oil

250g (9oz) button mushrooms, halved (or quartered if they are large)

Salt and freshly ground black pepper

2 small onions, sliced

4 cloves garlic, finely chopped

1.5kg (3lb 4oz) stewing beef, cut into 6cm (2in) chunks

150ml (5fl oz) red wine

1 tbsp chopped fresh thyme

1 tbsp red wine vinegar

650g (1½lb) floury potatoes, peeled and cut into 5mm (¼in) slices

25g (1oz) butter, diced

This is just the sort of rich and warming dish that is so popular in Ireland. It must be all the cold weather and, of course, all the rain. We shouldn't complain too much about the rain, because it's what makes the grass so green and produces such delicious and full-flavoured beef. Here, stewing cuts of beef are cooked long and slow with a full-bodied red wine and covered by potatoes, making this dish a convenient one-pot supper. You can even prepare it in advance and keep it covered, in the fridge, for up to 24 hours before cooking.

Preheat the oven to 150°C/ 300°F/Gas Mark 2.

Heat 3 tablespoons of the olive oil in a flameproof casserole dish over medium–high heat. Add the mushrooms, season with salt and pepper and toss for 2–3 minutes, until lightly golden. Remove the mushrooms from the dish with a slotted spoon and set aside.

If there isn't much oil left in the dish, add another tablespoon. Tip in the onions and garlic, stir over the heat, season with salt and pepper and cook for 4–5 minutes, until they start to turn golden at the edges. Add the meat and wine and 2 teaspoons of the thyme leaves. Bring to a boil and cover with a lid.

Bake in the oven for 1¼–1½ hours, until the meat is just tender. Take the dish out of the oven and turn up the heat to 230°C/450°F/ Gas Mark 8. Stir in the mushrooms and red wine vinegar. Arrange the potato slices over the beef in the dish (it's fine if there's more than one layer). Scatter over the remaining thyme and some salt and pepper, then dot with the butter.

Return the casserole dish to the (now hot) oven and bake for another 30–40 minutes, or until the potatoes are cooked through and beginning to turn golden. Bring to the table and serve.

Ballymaloe spiced beef

Serves 12–16

Preparation time: 20 minutes (plus 3–7 days to cure)

Cooking time: 2 to 3 hours

About 2kg (4lb 4oz) lean flank or silverside of beef

BALLYMALOE SPICE MIXTURE

100g (3½oz) Demerara or light brown sugar

125g (4½oz) salt

5g (¼oz) saltpetre (potassium nitrate)

25g (1oz) whole black peppercorns

25g (1oz) whole allspice (pimento or Jamaican pepper)

25g (1oz) whole juniper berries

Cucumber Pickles (page 133), to serve

Tomato Relish (page 20), to serve

Spiced beef used to be eaten all over Ireland at Christmas and New Year. In Cork, however, we eat spiced beef all year round and it is sold daily at the city's famous English Market. This spiced beef recipe has been passed down the Allen family and I think it's absolutely divine. In fact the first time I had spiced beef was when I came from Dublin to do the Cookery Course at Ballymaloe.

Spiced beef is useful to have in the fridge; it lasts for up to 6 weeks and is delicious thinly sliced and served with a little pickle and chutney. This recipe makes enough spice for this amount of beef. But if you have a smaller piece of beef, then use half of the mixture and keep the rest in a jar for 3 months.

Make the spice mixture by grinding all the ingredients (preferably in a spice grinder in a few batches) until fairly fine.

To prepare the beef, remove any bones and trim off any large pieces of fat (do keep some of the fat). Place the beef in an earthenware dish and rub the spice into every crevice of the beef. Leave in the fridge for 3–7 days, depending on the thickness of the meat. Turn it occasionally. (This is a dry spice, but after 1–2 days some liquid will come out of the meat.) The longer the meat is left in the spice, the longer it will last and the stronger the spiced flavour.

Jut before cooking the meat, roll and tie the meat neatly with cotton string into a compact shape, place in a large saucepan, cover with cold water and simmer for 2–3 hours (about 20 minutes per 450g/1lb) or until soft and cooked. When cooked you should be able to insert a skewer into the centre and the skewer will come out easily.

If you're serving the beef warm, remove from the liquid, then place on a carving board, cut away the string and carve into slices to serve. If the beef is to be eaten cold, remove it from the liquid, place in a high-sided dish, such as a roasting tin or gratin dish, cover it with a chopping board and weigh it down with four or five cans of tomatoes or beans (or something of a similar weight) and leave for 12 hours. After 12 hours, remove the board and weights. It will now keep in the fridge for up to 6 weeks. Serve by cutting into very thin slices and serving with cucumber pickle and tomato relish.

Cucumber pickle

Vegetarian

Makes about 5 x 300ml (11fl oz) jars

Ready in 1 hour

900g (2lb) cucumbers, unpeeled and very thinly sliced

1 medium red or white onion, thinly sliced

350g (12oz) sugar

1 tbsp salt

225ml (8fl oz) cider vinegar or white wine vinegar

Myrtle Allen started making this at Ballymaloe House more than 30 years ago. Not only is it good in burgers and all kinds of sandwiches, but it's wonderful with cold sliced meats and smoked fish, and it transforms a humble hard-boiled egg and a chunk of Cheddar into a feast. It's a pickle, so even though it will lose its vibrant green colour, it will keep for up to 3 months.

I like to use either a mandolin or a food processor to get very thin cucumber slices.

Mix the cucumber and onion in a large bowl. Add the sugar, salt and vinegar and mix well to combine. Make 1 hour ahead of when you want to use it, if possible.

Roast pheasant with wild mushroom, bacon and thyme stuffing

Serves 3–4

Preparation time: 10 minutes

Cooking time: 1½ hours

1 plump young pheasant, plucked and cleaned (or 1 chicken) (1–1.3kg/2–3lb)

Salt and fresh ground black pepper

40g (1½oz) butter

FOR THE STUFFING

40g (1½oz) butter

75g (3oz) bacon, cut into cubes (lardons) or dice about 1cm (½in) in size

½ medium onion, chopped

150g (5oz) wild mushrooms, sliced

1 clove garlic, mashed or finely grated

1½ tsp chopped fresh thyme

Salt and freshly ground black pepper

100g (3½oz) fresh breadcrumbs

FOR THE GRAVY

300ml (11fl oz) Chicken Stock (page 35)

Salt and fresh ground black pepper

Pheasant is a wonderful game bird. It's only available during the winter months' hunting season but it has such a rich, strong flavour that you wouldn't want it year-round. The stuffing uses another autumnal flavour, wild mushrooms. If you can't get wild mushrooms, then you could use button mushrooms, and the flavour will be almost as good.

Serve with Granny's Roasted Herbed Potatoes (page 158), Buttered Cabbage (page 144), Root Vegetable Mash (page 165) and plenty of gravy.

First make the stuffing. Melt half of the butter in a frying pan over medium heat. Add the bacon and cook for 3–4 minutes, stirring occasionally, until browned. Add the onion and cook for 5–6 minutes, stirring occasionally, until the onion is soft. Next add the mushrooms, garlic and thyme and season with salt and pepper. Increase the heat to high and cook for about 5 minutes, stirring occasionally, until the mushrooms have softened. Add the remaining butter and, when melted, stir in the breadcrumbs until they have soaked up the butter. Allow the stuffing to cool before stuffing the meat.

Preheat the oven to 190°C/375°F/Gas Mark 5.

Put the pheasant in a roasting tin, season the inside and outside with salt and pepper, then fill with the stuffing. Melt the butter in a saucepan over low heat. Add a piece of muslin cloth to soak, then wrap the pheasant completely in the muslin.

Roast in the oven for 1–1¼ hours. Test for doneness by inserting a skewer into the thigh; the juices should run clear and the legs will feel loose. Transfer the pheasant to a carving board, remove the muslin cloth and allow to rest while you make the gravy.

Place the roasting tin over medium heat and add the chicken stock to deglaze the tin. Bring to a simmer, using a wooden spoon to dislodge and dissolve any caramelised sticky pieces from the bottom of the tin. Taste for seasoning, then pour into a serving jug or gravy boat.

Carve the pheasant into slices and serve with the stuffing and gravy.

Vegetables and side dishes

A meal is only as good as its side dishes. A grand roast chicken, for example, should be served with crisp and golden roast potatoes that really do it justice. We Irish are a nation thoroughly in love with the potato, and whether roasted, boiled, mashed or fried there are few meals served without spuds. It is the floury varieties that are most popular here – varieties such as Kerr's Pink, Golden Wonder and Home Guards.

With so many delicious varieties available, vegetables needn't be an afterthought but can be just as delicious and impressive as the meat you serve. Cabbage, when cooked gently in butter – not overboiled – is a seriously special vegetable. Peas and broad beans make for beautiful and sweet summer treats. Both colcannon (page 170) and champ (page 169) are two divine examples of combining great fresh vegetables with our beloved mashed potatoes.

Lydia's salad with Shanagarry cream dressing

Vegetarian

Serves 2–4

Preparation time: 25 minutes

A few handfuls of lettuce leaves

4 tomatoes, quartered

½ cucumber, sliced

4 radishes, sliced

2 small beetroot, cooked, peeled and sliced

2 hard-boiled eggs, shelled and quartered

2 spring onions

2 tbsp chopped fresh parsley

A few sprigs of watercress

FOR THE SHANAGARRY CREAM DRESSING

2 hard-boiled eggs, shelled

1 tbsp dark brown sugar

Pinch of salt

1 tsp dry mustard powder

1 tbsp malt vinegar

125ml (4½fl oz) double or whipping cream

This salad comes from a Quaker lady, Lydia Strangman, who used to live in Kinoith, the house in which my husband grew up, on the grounds of the Ballymaloe Cookery School. It is wonderfully old-fashioned and salads of the sort would have been served all over the country in days gone by. To my husband Isaac, this is the perfect expression of a salad as comfort food.

The dressing is named after the small village of Shanagarry, which is just next to the Cookery School.

To make the dressing, cut the eggs in half and push the yolks through a sieve and into a bowl. Add the sugar, salt and mustard powder. Add the vinegar and cream and mix together. Chop the egg whites quite finely and stir half into the dressing mixture; reserve the rest for sprinkling over the salad.

You can arrange the salad on one large plate or on individual serving plates. Arrange the lettuce in the centre of the plate, then scatter over the tomatoes, cucumber, radishes and beetroot. Arrange the egg quarters on top, then sprinkle over the reserved egg whites, spring onions, parsley and watercress. Drizzle over the dressing and serve immediately.

Munster

Almost two-thirds of Ireland is farmed, and it is lush, green grass that dominates the landscape. Nowhere is the land more rich and fertile on this poetically named Emerald Isle than in the province of Munster. We're a nation of family farmers, and it's in this southerly part of the country that thousands of dairy farmers work the unrivalled land as their ancestors did before them. The farmers of Tipperary, Waterford and Cork know that grass-fed milk is liquid gold; they own the luxuriant land, the productive cows, and the valuable cooperatives that collect the milk. Between twice-daily milking, thousands of black and white cows graze these green lands, and the dairy produce from this corner of Ireland is exported all over the world. The availability of top-quality grass-fed milk has inspired a plethora of artisans who have brought the ancient tradition of cheese- and yogurt-making to modern Ireland.

Irish farmers have long known that transforming white liquid cream into thick, yellow butter is the best way to preserve this valuable source of fat over the winter months. The tradition of Irish country butter survives and thrives to this day: a gallon of milk is left at room temperature until the thick, delicious cream floats to the surface. This cream is scooped off, churned, separated from the buttermilk (which is used to make soda bread) and washed down with ice-cold water. A slab of butter is a must-have with an Irish dinner, and it's traditionally served in small, rounded balls known as 'pats'. Homemade country butter had other uses, too. It was thickly smeared over eggs just after they were laid to keep them fresh over the dark winter months when hens stop producing.

Pigs have long had a close affinity with Irish people. The backyard pig was 'the gentleman who paid the rent' because it provided much-needed income for tenants. Pigs were slaughtered at home, and no part of the animal was wasted; nothing, that is, apart from the grunt. Bacon was left to hang in the farmhouse chimney where it matured. Bacon and cabbage with parsley sauce is a favourite national dish (see page 144 for a variation). Nutritious fresh pig's blood was a precious resource that was not wasted either, and black pudding was its ideal home. It is fresh blood that gives black pudding its unctuous, silky texture – so good you should eat it with a spoon. Today, the resurgence of interest in fresh blood black pudding has captured the imaginations of butchers such as Jack McCarthy of Kanturk, County Cork, who produces award-winning pudding. Farmers such as Martin and Noreen Conroy of Woodside Farm, Cork, keep alive the tradition of rearing rare breed pigs outdoors, while Frank Murphy operates a small abattoir and butcher shop on Midleton's main street that dates back eight generations. Limerick was known as the 'City of Pigs', a nod to the thousands of people who were employed in local bacon factories. The county dish of Limerick is Packet and Tripe. Tripe (the lining of the sheep's stomach) is simmered with onion and milk, with cornflour added at the end to thicken. It's served piping hot with a portion of freshly congealed pig's blood, the packet.

Beef has always been a prized food, but it is only in recent times that prime cuts of beef have been served on Irish plates. Corned and spiced beef is a Cork speciality (see the recipe on page 132) and, like butter, it was a significant export product during the 17th century. Not for nothing was Cork city referred to as 'the slaughterhouse of Ireland'. Beef brisket, a cut from the lower chest, is submerged in a brine of water and salt, tied with a cotton string, and boiled with carrots, onions, peppercorns and mustard for 2 hours. Corned beef is traditionally served with cabbage, potatoes and mustard.

Salad dressings

Vegetarian

Makes 150ml (5fl oz)

Preparation time: 10 minutes

100ml (3½fl oz) extra virgin olive oil

50ml (2fl oz) freshly squeezed lemon juice

Pinch of salt and freshly ground black pepper

A great salad is often just as simple as some leaves with a dressing, but there are times when you might want to introduce other flavours and textures. Try adding chopped spring onions or red onions, diced avocado, olives, toasted pine nuts or roasted seeds, such as pumpkin, sunflower or sesame.

To dress the salad, drizzle a little dressing over the dry, washed leaves, then toss gently in a bowl. There should be just enough dressing so that the leaves are almost glistening; if they're overdressed, they will be soggy and heavy.

To make the dressing, mix the olive oil and lemon juice in a jar and shake vigorously to combine. Season to taste with salt and pepper. Alternatively, put the ingredients in a bowl and just stir together.

Variations
Honey garlic dressing: To the basic dressing, add 1 peeled and crushed small clove garlic, 1 teaspoon honey and 1 finely chopped small shallot (or ½ red onion).

Balsamic thyme vinaigrette: Replace the lemon juice with balsamic vinegar and add 1 teaspoon finely chopped thyme leaves to the basic dressing.

Dijon-honey vinaigrette: Replace the lemon juice with cider vinegar and add 1 teaspoon Dijon mustard and 1 teaspoon honey.

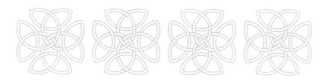

Cabbage with bacon and cream

Serves 6–8

Preparation time: 10 minutes

Cooking time: 10 minutes

50g (2oz) butter

6 rashers of smoked streaky bacon, thinly sliced

1 large savoy or green cabbage (about 600g/1lb 5oz), outer leaves removed

2 cloves garlic, crushed

1 tbsp water

200ml (7fl oz) single or double cream

Salt and freshly ground black pepper

This dish turns cabbage into something truly luxurious. The saltiness of the bacon works perfectly with cabbage. It is particularly good served with roast pork or chicken.

Melt the butter in a large frying pan or wok over high heat, add the bacon and fry for 4–5 minutes, until crisp and golden. Remove with a slotted spoon and drain on kitchen paper.

Meanwhile, cut the cabbage into quarters, removing the core from each piece, and thinly shred across the grain. Add the cabbage to the pan, along with the garlic and water. Sauté for about 5 minutes over medium–high heat, tossing frequently, until wilted and just tender.

Increase the heat a little and return the bacon to the pan. Pour in the cream and allow to bubble for a few minutes until thickened slightly. Season with salt and pepper to taste and serve immediately.

Buttered cabbage

Vegetarian

Serves 4–6

Preparation time: 5 minutes

Cooking time: 3 minutes

450g (1lb) savoy cabbage (or another dark green, leafy cabbage)

25g (1oz) butter

2 tbsp water

Salt and freshly ground black pepper

This is the way we prepare cabbage here at the Ballymaloe Cookery School. The cabbage isn't boiled, but cooked in butter with only a splash of water. This way the water doesn't leech out any flavour or nutrition.

Remove the tough outer leaves from the cabbage. Cut the head of cabbage into quarters, from top to bottom. Cut out the core, then slice the cabbage crossways into fine shreds, about 5mm (¼in) thick.

Combine the butter and water in a wide saucepan over medium heat and allow the butter to melt. Toss in the cabbage and season with salt and pepper. Cover with a lid and cook for 2–3 minutes, until just softened; do not let the cabbage burn. Taste immediately for seasoning and serve.

Buttered leeks

Vegetarian

Serves 4–6

Preparation time: 5 minutes

Cooking time: 10 minutes

6 medium leeks (about 1kg/2lb 2oz), washed and dark green tops and roots removed

25g (1oz) butter

2 tbsp water

Salt and freshly ground black pepper

2 tsp chopped fresh marjoram, chervil or tarragon (optional)

The leeks are cooked in butter and just a small amount of water, making them richly flavoured and wonderfully soft. The most mild of the allium family, leeks are very versatile, and this dish would be just as at home with chicken or pork as with a piece of fish.

Cut the leeks into slices about 2cm (¾in) thick.

Combine the butter and water in a saucepan over medium heat. Add the leeks, season with salt and pepper and stir to mix well. Reduce the heat to very low and cover. If you can, place a disc of greaseproof paper or butter wrapper on top of the leeks before you add the lid; this keeps them very moist though it isn't essential. Cook for 6–10 minutes, until just cooked; the leeks shouldn't lose their fresh green colour but should be good and soft. Stir in the chopped herbs (if using), then serve.

Creamed kale

Vegetarian

Serves 4

Preparation time: 5 minutes

Cooking time: 10 minutes

450g (1lb) curly kale, stems removed (approximately 300g/11oz without stems) and finely shredded

100ml (3½fl oz) single cream

25g (1oz) butter

Pinch of freshly grated nutmeg

Salt and freshly ground black pepper

Kale is a favourite of mine. It gets us through the dark winter months when there isn't much green around. This recipe is supremely soothing; the rich cream is offset by just a hint of warming nutmeg. It is a very versatile side dish and works well with roast or grilled meat.

Bring a large saucepan of salted water to a boil over high heat. Add the kale and cook for 3–5 minutes, just until tender, then drain the kale and return to the saucepan. Add the cream, butter and nutmeg and allow to bubble for 2–3 minutes, until slightly thickened. Season to taste with salt and pepper and serve while hot.

Pea purée

Vegetarian

Serves 4

Preparation time: 3 minutes

Cooking time: 2 minutes

Salt and freshly ground black
   pepper

450g (1lb) fresh or frozen peas

75ml (3fl oz) extra virgin olive oil

Good squeeze of lemon juice

Pea purée is naturally sweet and the green colour is lovely and intense. Make sure the peas are only just cooked, so they don't lose their bright colour and fresh flavour. This purée works especially well with fish, such as mackerel (page 87), but is great served as a dip with tortilla chips.

Bring a saucepan of water to a boil with 1 teaspoon salt. Tip in the peas and cook for 1–2 minutes (plus an extra minute for frozen peas), until just soft, then drain well. Combine with the olive oil and blend in a food processor or with a hand-held blender until smooth. Add lemon juice and salt and pepper to taste.

Minted broad beans

Vegetarian

Serves 2–4

Preparation time: 10 minutes

Cooking time: 5 minutes

Salt and freshly ground black
   pepper

500g (1lb 2oz) podded fresh or
   frozen broad beans

25g (1oz) butter

4 tbsp roughly chopped fresh mint

Broad beans are one of my favourite summer vegetables. Though a little time-consuming to prepare properly, they are always worth it. The mint here brings its fresh taste, which goes great with the beans, although you can just as easily serve them with parsley or no herbs at all. Keep the leftovers and toss into a salad the next day.

Bring a large saucepan of water to a boil with 1 teaspoon of salt. Add the beans, bring back to a boil and cook for 2–3 minutes if fresh, or 5–6 minutes if frozen. Drain well. Once cool enough to handle, pop the beans out of their skins.

Melt the butter in a small saucepan over medium heat. When the butter is frothing, add the beans and toss for 30–60 seconds to warm through. Add the mint, tossing it with the beans, and season well with salt and pepper. Spoon into a bowl and serve immediately.

Roast portabello mushrooms with lime cream cheese

Vegetarian

Serves 4

Preparation time: 5 minutes

Cooking time: 15 minutes

8 portabello mushrooms

2 tbsp extra virgin olive oil

25g (1oz) finely grated Parmesan cheese

2 cloves garlic, finely chopped

1 tsp chopped fresh thyme

Salt and freshly ground black pepper

FOR THE LIME CREAM CHEESE

150g (5oz) cream cheese, softened

1 heaped tbsp chopped fresh mint

Zest and juice of 1 lime

Juice of ½ lemon

Unsurprisingly, with all our rain and woodlands, we have an abundance of mushrooms every autumn. I love the big flat frills of a portabello mushroom – they look so proud and almost regal. If you can't get portabellos, any big flat mushroom would work well in this recipe.

Preheat the oven to 200°C/400°F/Gas Mark 6.

Remove the stems from the portabello mushrooms, arrange the caps on a baking tray, drizzle with the olive oil and sprinkle over the Parmesan cheese, garlic, thyme and some salt and pepper.

Roast for 10–15 minutes, until softened. Meanwhile, stir together the cream cheese, mint, lime zest and juice and lemon juice. Season with salt and pepper to taste.

Spoon the lime cream cheese on top of the mushrooms and serve.

Sticky cumin and apricot roast carrots and parsnips

Vegetarian

Serves 4–6

Preparation time: 10 minutes

Cooking time: 45 minutes

500g (1lb 2oz) small carrots, tops trimmed

500g (1lb 2oz) small parsnips, peeled and halved (if larger than the carrots)

3 tbsp extra virgin olive oil

1 tsp cumin seeds

Salt and freshly ground black pepper

2 tbsp apricot jam

2 tsp freshly squeezed lemon juice

1 tbsp chopped fresh coriander

We have great root vegetables and often I cook them simply roasted or in a mash with little dressing up. I do like to get more creative (especially by February when that's all there is growing!), and this dish is a real favourite of mine. The natural sugars in the vegetables work beautifully with the apricot jam.

Preheat the oven to 200°C/400°F/Gas Mark 6.

Combine the carrots and parsnips in a large roasting tin and drizzle with the olive oil. Scatter over the cumin seeds, season with salt and pepper and toss everything together to coat evenly. Roast in the oven for 40–45 minutes, tossing occasionally in the oil during cooking, until tender and golden.

In the meantime, heat the apricot jam and lemon juice for a few minutes in a small saucepan, stirring until you have a smooth, runny sauce. Pour this over the carrots and parsnips for the last 10 minutes of cooking, tossing the vegetables in the sauce to coat evenly. Sprinkle with the coriander just before serving.

Cauliflower cheese

Vegetarian

Serves 4–6

Preparation time: 5 minutes

Cooking time: 15 minutes

Salt and freshly ground black pepper

1 cauliflower, broken into small to medium florets, leaves reserved

300ml (11fl oz) Basic White Sauce (page 114) made with 3 tbsp plain flour and 3 tbsp butter

¼ tsp dry mustard powder

75g (3oz) grated cheese (Cheddar, Gruyère, Stilton, whatever you have!)

Good pinch of nutmeg (freshly grated, if possible)

1 tbsp chopped fresh parsley

Cauliflower cheese is maybe the most nostalgic dish to me. My mum would often make it when I was young. She'd mostly use whatever cheese was in the fridge, but usually a creamy cheese like a Cheddar. This is supremely comforting food to serve with roast chicken (see page 96) or beef.

Fill a large saucepan with about 3cm (1in) water and add a little salt. Arrange the cauliflower leaves in the bottom, sit the cauliflower florets on top, cover with a lid and bring to a boil. Cook for 8–10 minutes, until the stems are tender when pierced with a knife. Remove the cauliflower (discarding the leaves), drain well and arrange in a single layer in a large gratin dish.

In the meantime, make the cheese sauce. Start with the white sauce in a small saucepan over low heat and add the mustard and most of the grated cheese, reserving a little to scatter over the top of the dish, and stir until melted. Season to taste with salt, pepper and nutmeg.

Preheat the grill to high. Pour the sauce over the cauliflower in the dish and then scatter the reserved cheese on top. Grill for 2–3 minutes, until golden and bubbling on top. Scatter the chopped parsley over and serve.

Rachel's tip
Once the cauliflower cheese is assembled in the dish, it can be popped in the fridge for a few hours until you are ready to serve. Before grilling, reheat the cauliflower cheese in a preheated 200°C/400°F/Gas Mark 6 oven for about 20 minutes.

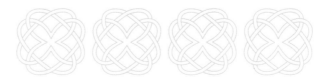

Granny's roasted herbed potatoes

Vegetarian (if made with olive oil)

Serves 4–6

Preparation time: 10 minutes

Cooking time: 1 hour

8–10 large floury potatoes, peeled and, if large, cut in half

Olive oil, duck or goose fat, or beef dripping

Salt

4 sprigs of thyme or 2 sprigs of rosemary

Some roast meats, like lamb or traditional stuffed chicken, simply demand really good roasted potatoes as an accompaniment. My late grandmother used to make the best roasted potatoes, the ones that are crispy and crunchy on the outside, and soft on the inside. The trick is to parboil the potatoes, then drain them and shake them in the saucepan before roasting.

Preheat the oven to 220°C/425°F/Gas Mark 7.

Drop the potatoes into boiling salted water and cook for 10 minutes. Drain off the water and shake the potatoes around in the dry saucepan with the lid on – this roughens the surface of the potatoes and makes them cook up crispier.

Heat a few tablespoons of olive oil in a roasting tin on top of the hob, add the potatoes and toss, making sure the potatoes are well coated (add more fat if they are not). Sprinkle with salt and roast in the hot oven for 35–55 minutes, basting (spooning the hot oil or fat over them) every now and then and turning over after 20 minutes or so. When they are nearly cooked, tuck the herb sprigs in between the potatoes. You can turn the oven down to 200°C/400°F/Gas Mark 6 after 15–20 minutes if you think they are dark enough. If the potatoes have to keep warm in the oven for any amount of time, do not cover them or they will go soggy.

Traditional herb stuffing

Makes about 250g (9oz)

Preparation time: 5 minutes

Cooking time: 10 minutes

25g (1oz) butter

1 tbsp extra virgin olive oil

1 onion, chopped

1 clove garlic, finely chopped

3 tbsp chopped mixed fresh herbs, such as parsley, thyme and sage

100g (3½oz) fresh white breadcrumbs

Salt and freshly ground black pepper

Stuffing may have once been used to bulk out more expensive meat, but it is cooked now as a delicious dish in its own right. This is a great basic stuffing recipe with lots of variations for you to try. Do experiment with your own favourite herbs and ingredients. This stuffing can be made in advance and kept in the fridge for a couple of days or frozen.

Combine the butter and olive oil in a saucepan over low heat. Add the onion and garlic, cover with a butter wrapper or a piece of greaseproof paper and then cover with a lid. Cook for 8–10 minutes, until the onions are soft but not browned. Take off the heat, remove the lid and paper cover and stir in the herbs and breadcrumbs. Season to taste with salt and pepper.

Variations

Lemony stuffing: (Makes about 250g/9oz)
Stir the finely grated zest of 1 lemon and the juice of ½ lemon into the stuffing mixture at the same time as the herbs and breadcrumbs (see above).

Chorizo stuffing: (Makes about 350g/12oz)
Cook 110g (4oz) very finely chopped dried chorizo sausage with the onion. Basil, thyme and marjoram would go well with this as the mixed herbs.

Smoked bacon stuffing: (Makes about 325g/11½oz)
Use a red onion in place of a yellow one, and cook with 50g (2oz) chopped smoked bacon or pancetta. Use thyme and/or parsley as the herbs.

Ivan Whelan's chestnut stuffing: (Makes about 450g/1lb)
Stir 150g (5oz) finely chopped and toasted chestnuts into the stuffing mixture. Use sage and/or rosemary as the herbs. For Christmas stuffing, add 50g (2oz) dried cranberries as well.

Fruit and nut stuffing: (Makes about 450g/1lb)
This variation goes surprisingly well with chicken. Stir 50g (2oz) chopped dried apricots, 50g (2oz) sultanas and 50g (2oz) chopped and toasted hazelnuts into the stuffing mixture.

Sautéed potatoes with caramelised onions

Vegetarian

Serves 4

Preparation time: 10 minutes

Cooking time: 40 minutes

800g (1¾lb) floury potatoes, peeled and cut into 2cm (¾in) cubes

4 tbsp extra virgin olive oil

Salt and freshly ground black pepper

25g (1oz) butter

1 large onion, thinly sliced

2 cloves garlic, finely chopped

2 tsp finely chopped fresh thyme or rosemary leaves

What I love about this recipe is that two humble ingredients are brought together, and with just a little effort they're made into something really special. The onions become golden and sweet in the pan, while the potatoes are crispy on the outside but wonderfully fluffy on the inside. This is delicious with any roast meat, a steak or even a burger. Use any leftover mixture in a frittata or omelette. You can omit the onions and just serve the sautéed potatoes, if you desire.

Dry the potatoes well in a clean tea towel. Pour 3 tablespoons of the olive oil into a large, heavy frying pan over high heat and add the potatoes. Turn the heat down to low–medium and sauté the potatoes for 30–35 minutes, tossing regularly, until softened, crisp and golden. Season well with salt and pepper.

In the meantime, heat the butter and remaining oil in a separate frying pan over low–medium heat. When the butter has melted, add the onion. Cook for about the same length of time, 30–35 minutes, until softened and caramelised to a golden colour. Add the garlic and thyme to the onions during the last 5 minutes of cooking and season well with salt and pepper.

Tip the caramelised onions into the pan with the sautéed potatoes, toss together and serve immediately.

Root vegetable mash

Vegetarian

Serves 4–6

Preparation time: 15 minutes

Cooking time: 20–25 minutes

1 carrot, cut into 2cm (¾in) chunks

Salt and freshly ground black pepper

1 parsnip, peeled and cut into 2cm (¾in) chunks

½ celeriac, peeled and cut into 2cm (¾in) chunks

1 sweet potato, peeled and cut into 2cm (¾in) chunks

2 tbsp butter or olive oil

2 tbsp double or whipping cream (optional)

1 tbsp chopped fresh parsley

1 tbsp chopped fresh thyme or rosemary

For a variation on standard mashed potato, why not try making it with other root vegetables? This recipe uses a mixture of parsnip, celeriac and sweet potato for a luxurious mash that's full of flavour. What's great about this side dish is that it works well with whatever root vegetables you have. This recipe should be considered a guideline only; try using more or less of any of the vegetables, or you could add Jerusalem artichokes, turnips or even beetroot. With butter and cream, you can turn modest ingredients into something quite luxurious.

Put the carrot in a large saucepan and cover with cold water, adding a good pinch of salt. Bring to a boil, then reduce the heat to medium–high and simmer for 5 minutes. Tip in the parsnip, celeriac and sweet potato and continue cooking for another 15 minutes, or until all the vegetables are tender.

Drain well, then add the butter and the cream (if using). Mash the vegetables either by hand or in a food processor for a smoother purée. Taste for seasoning, adding pepper and more salt if needed, then stir in the chopped herbs and serve.

Creamy mashed potato

Vegetarian

Serves 4

Preparation time: 10 minutes

Cooking time: 30 minutes

1kg (2lb 2oz) floury potatoes, scrubbed clean

Salt and freshly ground black pepper

50g (2oz) butter

200ml (7fl oz) milk, or 150ml (5fl oz) milk and 50ml (2fl oz) single or double cream, plus more if needed

Good mashed potato is the best comfort food ever, eaten on its own with a great knob of butter melting in it. It is hugely popular in our family – we'd eat it for every meal! For the most nutritious version – and the fluffiest mash – boil the potatoes in their skins and peel afterwards. Floury potatoes are always best as new potatoes are too waxy for mashing.

Put the potatoes in a large saucepan, cover with cold water and add a good pinch of salt. Bring the water to a boil and cook the potatoes for 10 minutes. Then pour out all but about 4cm (1½in) of the water, cover and continue to cook the potatoes over very low heat. Don't be tempted to stick a knife into them at any stage to see if they are cooked – the skins will split and the potatoes will just break up and become soggy if you do. About 20 minutes later, when you think the potatoes might be cooked, test them with a skewer; if they are soft, take them off the heat and drain them.

Peel the potatoes while they are still hot, holding them in a clean tea towel to avoid scalding your hands. Mash them immediately. Add the butter, but don't add any milk until the potatoes are free of lumps. Bring the milk to a boil in a small saucepan. Slowly stir the boiling milk into the potatoes – you may not need it all, or you may need more, depending on the texture of the potatoes. Season to taste with salt and pepper.

Rachel's tip
If you want to make the mash in advance, add a little extra milk, to keep the potatoes moist as they sit. The mash keeps well in a warm oven as long as it is covered with a lid, plate or foil.

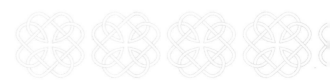

Boxty

Vegetarian

Serves 4

Preparation time: 5 minutes

Cooking time: 20 minutes

1 egg

50ml (2fl oz) single cream

250g (9oz) floury potatoes, peeled and coarsely grated

15g (½oz) plain flour

Salt and freshly ground black pepper

25g (1oz) butter

Boxty are traditional potato pancakes that are particularly loved in the Northern counties. They can be served as a potato side dish rather than mashed or boiled potatoes or as part of an Irish breakfast (page 108). This is my husband Isaac's take on boxty, he uses cream and not too much flour so they're good and rich.

In a bowl, whisk together the egg with the cream. Add the potato and flour, season with salt and pepper and stir to mix. The mixture will be slightly runny.

Melt the butter in a frying pan over medium heat. Add the potato mixture and cook for 8–10 minutes on each side, until the surface is golden brown and the potato is cooked through. Remove to a serving plate and cut into wedges to serve.

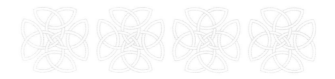

Pea and spring onion champ

Vegetarian

Serves 6–8

Preparation time: 10 minutes

Cooking time: 40 minutes

1.5kg (3lb 4oz) floury potatoes,
  scrubbed clean

Salt and freshly ground black
  pepper

100g (3½oz) butter

500ml (18fl oz) milk or 400ml
  (14fl oz) milk and 100ml (3½fl oz)
  single cream

450g (1lb) fresh or frozen peas

75g (3oz) sliced spring onions

4 tbsp chopped fresh parsley

Champ is similar to colcannon, but made with spring onions. I've added peas for their sweetness and to make this dish a little more substantial. The peas and spring onions are cooked in the milk so their flavour infuses the whole dish. This champ makes a versatile side dish and goes well with any meat, especially bacon or pork.

Fill a large saucepan with water, then add the potatoes and a good pinch of salt. Bring to a boil and boil for 10 minutes. Then pour all but about 4cm (1½in) of the water out of the pan, cover and continue to cook the potatoes over very low heat. (Don't be tempted to stick a knife into them as the skins will break and they will disintegrate.) Continue to cook for another 20–30 minutes, until a skewer goes in easily.

Drain the potatoes, peel while they are still hot and put into a bowl along with three-quarters of the butter. Mash immediately by hand, or beat in an electric food mixer fitted with the paddle attachment, until they are free of lumps.

Bring the milk (or milk and cream) to a boil in a small saucepan. Add the peas and spring onions and boil for 2 minutes. Then add the parsley and remove from the heat. Add most of this mixture to the potatoes, season with salt and pepper and beat until creamy and smooth. Add more of the milk mixture if necessary (you might not need all of it, but do add in all of the peas and spring onions using a slotted spoon), then serve hot with the remaining butter melting in the centre.

Roast garlic colcannon

Vegetarian

Serves 4–6

Preparation time: 15 minutes

Cooking time: 1¼ hours

1 large bulb garlic, left whole and unpeeled

2 tbsp extra virgin olive oil

Salt and ground black pepper

1 sprig of rosemary

1kg (2lb 2oz) floury potatoes, scrubbed clean

450g (1lb) savoy cabbage or kale

250ml (9fl oz) milk

50g (2oz) butter, plus extra to serve

Colcannon is a traditional Irish dish made from mashed potato and cabbage or kale. By roasting the garlic, its flesh is tempered and tamed to become sweet and mellow.

Preheat the oven to 220°C/425°F/Gas Mark 7.

Place the whole bulb of garlic in a small ovenproof dish, drizzle with the olive oil, season with salt and pepper and add the sprig of rosemary. Cover with foil and roast for about 45 minutes, until the garlic has completely softened.

Put the potatoes in a large saucepan and cover with cold water. Add a good pinch of salt, cover with a lid and bring to a boil. After 10 minutes, strain off two-thirds of the water, put the lid back on the pan and cook over gentle heat so that the potatoes steam for about 30 minutes, until they are tender.

Remove and discard the dark tough outer leaves from the cabbage (if using). Wash the rest and cut into quarters, removing the core. Cut the cabbage across the grain into slices about 5mm (¼in) thick. Place in another large saucepan, add the milk, and simmer for about 4 minutes or until tender. If you're using kale, cut out the tough centre rib of the leaves, then slice and cook in milk as for the cabbage.

When the potatoes are just cooked, peel them while still warm and immediately mash with the butter and some salt and pepper. Use your fingers to squeeze out the roasted garlic pulp and beat into the potatoes with enough boiling milk from the cabbage to make a fluffy purée. Then drain the cooked cabbage or kale, stir into the mash and taste for seasoning.

For perfection, serve immediately in a hot dish with a lump of butter melting on top.

Puddings and cakes

A truly delicious pudding can really make a meal. Since I was a young girl I have always enjoyed making puddings. I do have a real sweet tooth and, even if it's just a morsel, I crave a little something sweet after my meal.

The puddings and cakes in Ireland often feature the fruits we can grow here, which means tarts and crumbles packed full of our gorgeous apples, pears and lots of lovely berries. There are also more specifically Irish dishes such as Carrageen Moss Pudding (page 197). This chapter also includes a few recipes that use the delicious flavours of Irish coffee, and there's also a recipe for the drink itself (page 210).

Darina's summer pudding

Vegetarian

Serves 12–16

Preparation time: 30 minutes

Cooking time: 30 minutes

Ready in 8 hours

2 (18cm/7in) sponge cakes
(see page 176)

550g (1lb 4oz) caster sugar

725ml (24fl oz) water

225g (8oz) blackcurrants, fresh
or frozen

225g (8oz) redcurrants, fresh
or frozen

225g (8oz) raspberries, fresh
or frozen

225g (8oz) strawberries, fresh
or frozen

Vanilla ice cream or softly whipped
cream, to serve

This is my mother-in-law Darina's recipe, which we teach in the Cookery School. It's such a celebration of summer berries, their flavours mixing and melding together as the pudding sets in the fridge. This summer pudding uses cake rather than bread to line the bowl. That extra dimension of sweetness makes it really special and it should be served with lots of softly whipped cream.

Make sure the fruit and syrup is boiling when you pour it into the cake-lined bowl, otherwise the syrup won't properly soak in. You can use either fresh or frozen berries.

Cut each round of sponge cake in half, horizontally. Set aside one of the halves for topping the pudding.

Line a large bowl with cake in a single layer. A plastic bowl is useful because it can be squeezed to make unmoulding easier, but it's not essential; use whatever large bowl you have. The softer side of the cake should be against the bowl. You will need to cut the cake halves into a few pieces to make a sort of patchwork of cake with which to line the bowl. I try and use a few large pieces to begin with then make up the lining by cutting smaller pieces from the remaining cake halves. When you are done, the bowl should be lined with a single layer of cake going all the way up the sides but you will have some scraps left over. Reserve these scraps for later, along with the reserved cake half. Place the cake-lined bowl in a gratin or baking dish.

Combine the sugar and water in a saucepan over medium heat, stirring to dissolve the sugar, and bring to a boil. Boil for 2 minutes, then add the blackcurrants and redcurrants and cook until the fruit bursts, 3–4 minutes. Stir in the raspberries and strawberries and remove from the heat.

Ladle some of the hot syrup and fruit into the sponge-cake-lined bowl. When about half full, add the remaining scraps of cake, then fill right up to the top of the bowl with the rest of the fruit (using a slotted spoon) and some more of the syrup. Reserve any excess syrup and place in the fridge. Cover the pudding with the reserved cake half, making a lid for it all, the juice may overflow a little (that's what the gratin or baking dish is for). Put a plate right side up on top

recipe continues overleaf

and press down with a heavy weight (such as two cans of tomatoes or beans); more juice will overflow. Allow to cool, then place in the fridge for at least 8 hours or overnight (but it will keep for 3–4 days).

To serve, turn the pudding upside down onto a deep serving dish, unmould by gently squeezing the bowl to free the pudding, then lift the bowl off. Pour any leftover syrup over the top. Serve with vanilla ice cream or softly whipped cream.

Sponge cake

Vegetarian

Makes 2 (18cm/7in) layers

Preparation time: 15 minutes

Cooking time: 25 minutes

125g (4½oz) butter, softened

175g (6oz) caster sugar

3 eggs

175g (6oz) plain flour

1 tsp baking powder

1 tbsp milk

Preheat the oven to 180°C/350°F/Gas Mark 4.

Use a little butter to grease two (18cm/7in) cake tins, then sprinkle with a little flour and line the bottom of each with a round of parchment paper.

In a bowl, using a wooden spoon or an electric food mixer fitted with a paddle attachment, cream the butter. Gradually add the sugar, beating until soft and light and quite pale in colour. Add the eggs, one at a time, and beat well between each addition. Sift in the flour and baking powder, then mix everything together lightly and add the milk to moisten. Divide the mixture evenly between the two cake tins and make a little dip in the centre of each to ensure an even rise.

Bake for 20–25 minutes, until a skewer inserted into the middle comes out clean. Place on a wire rack to cool.

Fluffy lemon pudding

Vegetarian

Serves 6

Preparation time: 15 minutes

Cooking time: 40 minutes

50g (2oz) butter, softened

250g (9oz) caster sugar

3 eggs, separated

75g (3oz) plain flour

300ml (11fl oz) milk

Finely grated zest and juice of
2 lemons

Icing sugar, for dusting

When cooked, this delectable pudding has a layer of lemon sponge sitting on top of a pool of hot lemon curd. This has been made at Ballymaloe for years because it is a favourite of so many people.

Preheat the oven to 180°C/350°F/Gas Mark 4.

Beat the butter by hand in a large bowl or with an electric food mixer fitted with the paddle attachment until it is really soft and creamy. Add the sugar and beat until pale and fluffy. Add the egg yolks, one at a time, beating each one in before adding the next. Sift in the flour and add the milk and lemon zest and juice, and mix well together.

Whisk the egg whites in a large, spotlessly clean bowl until they form stiff peaks. Gently fold the egg whites into the cake mixture until well mixed. Pour the mixture into a 1.2 litre (2 pint) oval pie dish (18 x 23cm/7 x 9in) with 5cm (2in) sides.

Bake for 30–40 minutes, until golden and set on top, but not set underneath. Remove from the oven and allow to cool slightly before sprinkling with icing sugar and serving.

Variation
Individual puddings: Use six small to medium ramekins or ovenproof cups arranged on a baking tray and bake for 15–20 minutes, or until just set. Serve as above.

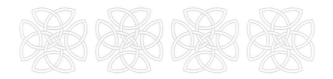

Fruit tarts

Vegetarian

Serves 8–10

Preparation time: 30 minutes

Cooking time: 50 minutes

Ready in 1½ hours

175g (6oz) butter, softened

50g (2oz) caster sugar, plus extra for sprinkling

2 eggs

250g (9oz) plain flour, plus extra for dusting

Fruit filling (see page 182)

Softly whipped cream or custard

A seasonal fruit tart is one of the mainstays of Irish puddings. It could be filled with apples and blackberries in the autumn, gooseberries in the summer or rhubarb in the spring. Many Irish farmhouses grow fruit, and it always find its way into a tart of this sort. The pastry isn't fancy, just a simple but delicious buttery pastry, similar to one that Mrs. O'Connell, my husband's late grandmother, used to make. My mother-in-law always insists on serving puddings like this with softly whipped cream and with a good sprinkling of brown sugar. It's really worth doing; the cream accentuates the sweetness of the tart, a little like sprinkling salt over a savoury dish.

To make the pastry, use a hand-held beater or an electric food mixer fitted with a dough hook attachment and cream the butter and sugar together until pale and creamy. Add one egg, beating continuously. Beat the second egg in a separate bowl. Pour half of it into the mixture (reserving the remainder for later) and beat again. Sift over the flour and stir in gently to make a smooth, soft dough. Tip the dough onto a clean work surface and knead a little before dividing in two. Shape each piece into a flat round, cover with cling film and leave in the fridge for at least 1 hour.

Preheat the oven to 180°C/350°F/Gas Mark 4. Lightly butter a 23cm (9in) tart tin or shallow pie dish.

Place each pastry half on a floured work surface and roll out to a thickness of about 3mm (⅛in). Use one piece to line the tin, trimming off the excess pastry with the back of a knife. Brush a little of the reserved beaten egg around the edge of the pastry.

Add your chosen fruit filling (see overleaf) to the pastry and top with the second rolled-out piece of pastry, trimming the excess once again and pressing the edges together to seal. Use any leftover pastry to decorate the top by rolling it out and cutting it into shapes. Brush all over with the remaining beaten egg.

Bake for 45–50 minutes, until the fruit is tender when tested with a skewer and the pastry is golden. Remove from the oven, lightly sprinkle with sugar and allow to cool slightly. Cut into wedges and serve with whipped cream or custard.

recipe continues overleaf

Fruit fillings

Apple: Peel, core and dice 700g (1½lb) Bramley or other cooking apples and toss with 150g (5oz) granulated sugar and 2–3 cloves.

Plum, nectarine or peach: Halve, pit and quarter 900g (2lb) plums, nectarines or peeled peaches and toss with 75g (3oz) caster or granulated sugar and 2 tablespoons cornflour. Add an additional teaspoon of the cornflour if the fruit is very ripe.

Strawberry: Toss 700g (1½lb) hulled strawberries (halved if large) with 1 tablespoon cornflour and 50g (2oz) caster or granulated sugar.

Custard

Vegetarian

Makes 700ml (24fl oz)

Preparation time: 5 minutes

Cooking time: 15 minutes

500ml (18fl oz) milk

5 egg yolks

100g (3½oz) caster sugar

Custard is the perfect accompaniment for a fruit tart or crumble (pages 180 and 190). This recipe takes me right back to my childhood.

Pour the milk into a large saucepan and slowly bring to a boil. Meanwhile, beat the egg yolks and sugar together in a large bowl until pale and thick. Gradually whisk the hot milk into the beaten eggs and sugar and pour the whole mixture back into the saucepan.

Return to low heat and cook gently for 5–8 minutes, stirring all the time, until the custard thickens slightly (it should just coat the back of the spoon). Pour into a warm jug to serve. If reheating, do so very gently over low heat so that the eggs don't scramble.

Variations

Vanilla custard: Add 1 vanilla pod, split, to the milk when bringing to a boil in the pan. Remove the pod from the custard before pouring it into the jug to serve. Yummy with plum or rhubarb crumble (page 192).

Orange custard: Add 1 strip of orange zest to the milk when bringing to a boil in the pan. Remove the zest from the custard before pouring it into the jug to serve. Goes especially well with the Steamed Ginger Treacle Pudding (page 214).

Irish apple cake

Vegetarian

Serves 4–6

Preparation time: 30 minutes

Cooking time: 50 minutes

Ready in 1½ hours

225g (8oz) plain flour

½ tsp baking powder

100g (3½oz) butter

100g (3½oz) sugar, plus 2 tbsp

1 egg, beaten

Approximately 100ml (3½fl oz) milk

1 large cooking apple, about 300g (11oz) in weight

1 tsp ground cinnamon

Softly whipped cream, to serve

This wonderful cake is a delicious way to make the most of the autumn apples. My husband's grandmother, Myrtle Allen, has been making this for many years, and it is still made today at Ballymaloe.

Preheat the oven to 180°C/350°F/Gas Mark 4. Butter a 25cm (10in) pie dish.

Mix the flour with the baking powder. Rub in the butter with your fingertips until the texture resembles breadcrumbs. Add the 100g sugar, beaten egg and enough milk to form a soft dough. Pat out half of the dough in the greased pie dish (don't worry – it is supposed to be very wet).

Peel, core and chop the apple into 2cm (¾in) cubes. Arrange the apples on the dough and sprinkle with 1 tablespoon sugar and the cinnamon. Gently spoon out the remaining dough on top of the apples to cover them completely. Sprinkle with the remaining sugar and cut a slit through the middle of the top dough.

Bake for 40–50 minutes, until golden and crunchy on the outside (the apples should be soft on the inside). Serve with softly whipped cream.

Rachel's tip
If the butter is cold (just taken from the fridge), grate it into the flour and it will rub in within a couple of seconds.

Connacht

Connacht is renowned for its dramatic, cloud-capped mountains and glacial lakes, its wet bog land and indented coastline. Small villages pepper the region and it is here, in the public houses, that farmers and fishermen gather with the locals over a pint. Depending on the vagaries of the weather, the mighty Atlantic Ocean gently soothes or vigorously batters the majestic western coast of this captivating province, which encompasses Galway, Mayo, Sligo, Leitrim and Roscommon.

Overlooking the wild Atlantic seas in North Mayo is the Céide Fields. It was here, nearly 6,000 years ago, that Stone Age communities produced food from the land. In the 1930s, vestiges of ancient field systems were discovered beneath a blanket of peat, along with evidence of dwellings and cultivated fields of wheat and barley. The skills from these early Mayo farmers have been handed down through the generations, and farmers across these scenic counties continue to work the land today.

The abundant rain, aided by the warm Gulf Stream, creates the optimum climate for grass to grow in these wet, warm, western fields. Unsurprisingly, cattle favour this nutritious and bountiful food. Cows have pervaded the Irish psyche for centuries – the Irish for road, bóthar, translates as 'cow-track' and an 8th-century Irish text boasts of high-quality marbled meat from cattle fed nothing but 'full new milk and liugfér' (newly mown grass) as calves. Today, the offspring of spring-calving cows suckle their mothers' milk for nine months before weaning to grass. Suckler herds of Angus, Hereford, Limousin, Charolais, Simmental and Belgian Blue breeds produce world-class Irish beef. Native Irish rare breeds such as Dexter, Irish Moiled and Droimeann cattle can be seen grazing the stone-walled fields of Connacht, too.

The rocky, rough uplands are more suited to hardy sheep such as the Blackface mountain breed, which dates back to the 1800s. The moist Atlantic sea spray finds its way to the Connemara fields where these sheep graze, and this salty mist enhances the growth of the wild grasses, heathers, herbs and flowers. The result is Connemara Hill lamb, a meat that is imbued with sweet and salty flavours and is considered so unique that a sought-after stamp from European authorities ensures that only lamb produced on these majestic mountains can be labelled as 'Connemara Hill lamb'. For many people, it is lamb that is the core ingredient in Irish stew (see the recipe on page 80), and you will not find a finer-tasting meat than young sheep reared on the sweet grasses of the Connemara hills.

The revered Atlantic salmon is enshrined in Irish mythology and folklore, and also in the history of Irish food. Fishermen and locals await late autumn with excitement and anticipation, for this is the time of the salmon run. Hordes of agile salmon return from the salty ocean and enter their natal freshwater rivers to spawn. In the 1700s, salmon was roasted over the rising smoke of the turf fire; in recent history, a whole salmon was seasoned and then tightly wrapped in sheets of yesterday's newspaper and cooked over an open fire. Today, artisans such as the Roberts family, who own and run the oldest smokehouse in Connemara, ensure that the tradition of hand-filleting and hand-smoking salmon continues.

Sweet scones with blueberry jam

Vegetarian

Makes 10 scones and 2 x 300ml (11fl oz) jars of jam

Preparation time: 40 minutes

Cooking time: 30 minutes

Ready in 45 minutes

450g (1lb) plain flour

Pinch of salt

20g (¾oz) baking powder

25g (1oz) caster sugar

75g (3oz) butter, softened

2 eggs

200ml (7fl oz) milk

FOR THE JAM

375g (13oz) blueberries, fresh or frozen

2 tbsp water

300g (11oz) caster sugar

3 tbsp freshly squeezed lemon juice

FOR A CRUNCHY GLAZE (OPTIONAL)

1 small egg, beaten (if there is no liquid left from the scones)

Granulated sugar

Butter, whipped cream or clotted cream, to serve

Afternoon tea just wouldn't be right without scones! They are so simple and delicious, particularly with homemade jam, which is much easier to make than many people realise. This scone recipe comes from Elizabeth O'Connell, Isaac's maternal grandmother.

First make the jam, which will then keep in a cool place for several months. Place a saucer in the fridge for testing the jam later. To sterilise the jars (any shape will do, preferably with a lid), put them through a dishwasher cycle, boil in a pan of water for 5 minutes, or place in a preheated oven (150°C/300°F/Gas Mark 2) for 10 minutes.

Combine the blueberries and water in a saucepan over medium heat. Bring to a boil and mash the fruit with a potato masher. Add the sugar and lemon juice and stir over high heat for 5 minutes. Test by placing a small blob on the chilled saucer, leave for 20 seconds, and run your finger through the blob. If it forms a skin, the jam is set. Carefully remove the jars from the dishwasher, pan or oven, using oven gloves, if necessary. Pour the jam into the jars immediately and cover with their lids and screwbands.

To make the scones, preheat the oven to 230°C/450°F/Gas Mark 8. Lightly flour a baking tray.

Sift the flour, salt and baking powder into a large bowl; add the sugar and mix. Rub in the butter and make a well in the centre. In another bowl, whisk the eggs and then add the milk. Pour all but 60ml (2½fl oz) of this liquid into the dry ingredients and, using one hand, mix to a soft dough, adding more of the liquid, if necessary.

Turn out onto a floured work surface and knead until a dough is formed. Sprinkle with flour and gently roll out until it is 2–5cm (¾–2in) thick. Cut with a knife or a round 5cm (2in) cutter into scones. Place on the prepared baking tray.

If you opt for a crunchy glaze, brush the scones with the liquid left in the bowl or with a beaten egg, then dip each one, wet side down, into the granulated sugar. Return to the baking tray, sugared side up.

Bake in the centre of the oven for 7–10 minutes, until golden brown on top. Cool on a wire rack. Serve split with butter and jam or with jam and a blob of whipped cream or clotted cream.

Fruit crumbles

Vegetarian

Serves 6

Preparation time: 15 minutes

Cooking time: 40 minutes

Ready in 2 hours

Fruit filling (see below and overleaf)

75g (3oz) butter, diced

150g (5oz) plain flour

75g (3oz) soft light brown sugar

Icing sugar, for dusting

Lightly whipped cream, ice cream
  or custard (page 182), to serve

A fruit crumble is a divine yet simple pudding. It's one of the first pudding recipes we teach here at the Ballymaloe Cookery School. Once you know the technique for making the topping, you can use it to cover whatever fruit you have on hand. I love to serve this dish with flavoured homemade custard (page 182).

Preheat the oven to 180°C/350°F/Gas Mark 4. Lightly butter a 1 litre (1¾ pint) oval (15 x 20cm/6 x 8in) pie dish with 5cm (2in) sides or six individual 120ml (4½fl oz) ramekins. Set on a baking tray.

Prepare your choice of fruit filling from the following list and spread evenly in the bottom of the pie dish or ramekins.

To make the crumble topping, rub the flour and butter together in a large bowl until it resembles very coarse breadcrumbs (don't rub it in too much or the crumble won't be crunchy once cooked). Stir in the sugar. Sprinkle the topping over the fruit. (At this point you can place the crumble in the fridge for up to 48 hours or freeze until you want to bake it.)

Bake the crumble for 35–40 minutes in the pie dish (15–20 minutes in the ramekins), until golden and bubbly. Serve dusted with icing sugar and with a dollop of lightly whipped cream.

Fruit fillings

Apple and raspberry: Cook 600g (1lb 5oz) (about 2) peeled, cored and roughly chopped cooking apples (such as Bramley or Granny Smith) with 50g (2oz) caster or granulated sugar and 1 tablespoon of water for 6–8 minutes, until soft. Spoon into the prepared pie dish and sprinkle over 200g (7oz) fresh or frozen raspberries.

Apple and sweet mincemeat: Cook 3–4 (800g/1¾lb) peeled, cored and roughly chopped cooking apples (such as Bramley or Granny Smith) with 75g (3oz) caster or granulated sugar and 2 tablespoons of water for 6–8 minutes, or until just softened. Toss with 110g (4oz) sweet mince pie filling and spoon into the prepared pie dish.

recipe continues overleaf

Strawberry and rhubarb: Cook 450g (1lb) rhubarb, roughly chopped, with 75g (3oz) sugar and 1 tablespoon of water for about 5 minutes, until it begins to soften. Spoon into the prepared pie dish and sprinkle over 225g (8oz) hulled and quartered strawberries.

Plum and vanilla: Dissolve 75g (3oz) caster or granulated sugar in 100ml (3½fl oz) red wine (or water) in a saucepan over low heat. Pit and quarter 600g (1lb 5oz) plums. Add to the pan with 1 split vanilla pod and cook for 5 minutes, or until the plums begin to soften. Spoon the plums into the prepared pie dish with a slotted spoon. Simmer the remaining liquid until it has reduced by half, making a thick syrup. Remove the vanilla pod and drizzle the syrup over the plums before topping with the crumble.

Variations
Sugars: In place of the light brown sugar, use Demerara, caster or granulated sugar in the crumble topping.

Topping texture: When adding the sugar, stir in any of these: 25g (1oz) rolled oats; 75g (3oz) chopped pecans, chopped hazelnuts or flaked almonds; 2 teaspoons of ground spices, such as cinnamon, nutmeg or mixed spice.

Rachel's tip
Keep a large batch of the crumble mixture in a food bag in the freezer. Even when frozen, it will easily crumble, so you can remove handfuls to use straight away as you need it.

Rhubarb and ginger bread and butter pudding

Vegetarian

Serves 4–6

Preparation time: 30 minutes

Cooking time: 50 minutes

Ready in 2 hours

450g (1lb) rhubarb stalks, cut into 1cm (½in) slices

4 tsp finely grated fresh ginger

150g (5oz) caster sugar

50g (2oz) butter, softened

12 slices white sandwich bread, crusts removed

350ml (12fl oz) single or double cream

350ml (12fl oz) milk

4 eggs

Pinch of salt

2 tbsp granulated sugar

Icing sugar, to serve

Softly whipped cream, to serve

This variation on the classic bread and butter pudding uses rhubarb and ginger, which go together so well. You can use fresh or frozen rhubarb and enjoy the pudding year-round.

For me and so many people in Ireland, this is the absolute essence of comfort food: a pudding that brings us all back to our childhoods, to memories of a dish that is best when cooked without precision or fussiness. It is unashamedly indulgent – the bread soaks up the custard while the sprinkling of granulated sugar ensures the top is perfectly crisp.

Rhubarb is something that grows really well in Ireland, and I have quite a prolific patch in my garden. I like to stew it simply with sugar and water, then serve it with yogurt or custard. This pudding is a serious treat.

Scatter the rhubarb in a 25cm (10in) square ovenproof baking dish, and sprinkle with half the grated ginger and half the caster sugar. Toss together and then let sit for about 30 minutes to soften a little.

Preheat the oven to 180°C/350°F/Gas Mark 4. Butter the bread and arrange four slices, buttered side down, in the baking dish. Scatter over half of the prepared rhubarb and top with four more slices of bread, again buttered side down. Repeat with the remaining rhubarb mixture and bread.

Combine the cream, milk and remaining grated ginger in a saucepan and bring just to a boil. While this is coming to a boil, whisk the eggs, salt and remaining caster sugar in a bowl. Continuing to whisk, pour the hot liquid into the egg mixture until well mixed. Slowly pour this custard over the bread and let soak for 10 minutes. Sprinkle the granulated sugar over the top.

Place the baking dish in a deep-sided roasting tin and pour in enough boiling water to come halfway up the sides (making a bain-marie). Carefully place in the oven and bake for 45–50 minutes, until the pudding feels just set in the centre. Serve warm with a light dusting of icing sugar and whipped cream.

Carrageen moss pudding with poached rhubarb

Vegetarian
Serves 4–6
Preparation time: 15 minutes
Cooking time: 20 minutes
Ready in 2½ hours

7g (¼oz) or 1 fistful carrageen (Irish moss) (don't use too much or the pudding will be too firm and strong in flavour)

900ml (1½ pints) milk

50g (2oz) caster sugar

1 egg, separated

1 tsp vanilla extract

100ml (3½fl oz) water

225g (8oz) granulated sugar

450g (1lb) rhubarb, stalks trimmed and cut into 2cm (¾in) chunks

I was first introduced to carrageen (carraigín in Irish, meaning 'little rock') moss pudding – Irish moss pudding – when I came down to Ballymaloe at the age of eighteen. Myrtle Allen, who first opened the Ballymaloe House in 1964, has been cooking this dish in the restaurant for decades. It is an old Irish dish but hers is undoubtedly the best version I've tried. Carrageen is a type of seaweed that works like gelatin, and it gently sets the cooked milk to make a light and fluffy pudding. Carrageen is harvested at low tide, then put out to dry on the rocks. High in iodine and vitamins, it is also used in a traditional recipe for cough syrup that Myrtle Allen still makes and that she swears by. You can buy carrageen in health food shops and online.

Soak the carrageen in lukewarm water for 10 minutes, then drain and combine in a saucepan with the milk. Bring to a boil, then simmer over very low heat for 20 minutes.

Pour the milk through a sieve into a bowl. The carrageen will now be swollen and resembling a jellyfish, so push the jelly through the sieve into the milk. Discard the remaining carrageen. Whisk in the caster sugar, egg yolk and vanilla.

Whisk the egg white until stiff and gently stir it into the milk; it will rise to give the pudding a light, fluffy top. Pour into one large bowl or evenly distribute into individual cups or glasses. Cover and place in the fridge for 1–2 hours to set.

To poach the rhubarb, combine the water and granulated sugar in a saucepan, stir and bring to a boil. Add the rhubarb, cover, bring to a boil and simmer for exactly 1 minute. Turn off the heat and allow the rhubarb to remain in the covered saucepan until almost cool. Transfer to a bowl to finish cooling.

Serve the rhubarb on top of or on the side of the carrageen pudding.

Porter cake

Vegetarian

Serves 10–12

Preparation time: 30 minutes

Cooking time: 2 hours

Ready in 3 hours

450g (1lb) plain flour

1 tsp grated or ground nutmeg

1 tsp mixed spice

1 tsp baking powder

Pinch of salt

225g (8oz) butter

225g (8oz) light brown sugar

450g (1lb) sultanas or raisins or a mixture of both

75g (3oz) chopped candied peel, shop-bought or homemade (see page 202)

2 eggs

1 x 330ml (12oz) bottle porter or stout

This traditional Irish cake uses a porter, such as Guinness, Beamish or Murphy's, and is a deliciously rich and moist fruit cake. Make it a few days in advance of the celebratory event (it's perfect for St. Patrick's Day) if you wish, and it will improve even more!

Preheat the oven to 180°C/350°F/Gas Mark 4. Line the sides and bottom of a 20cm (8in) high-sided round cake tin (the sides should be about 7cm/2¾in high) with greaseproof paper.

Sift the flour, nutmeg, spice, baking powder and salt into a bowl. Rub in the butter, then stir in the brown sugar, sultanas and candied peel.

Whisk the eggs in another bowl and add the porter. Pour into the dry ingredients and mix well. Pour into the prepared tin.

Bake for about 2 hours. If the cake starts to brown too quickly on top, cover it with foil or greaseproof paper after about 1 hour. The cake is done when a skewer inserted into the centre comes out clean. Allow the cake to sit in the tin for about 20 minutes before turning it out and leaving it to cool on a wire rack.

Christmas pudding with whiskey cream

Vegetarian

Serves 8–12

Preparation time: 40 minutes

Cooking time: 3 hours

Ready in 5 hours

100g (3½oz) raisins

100g (3½oz) sultanas

100g (3½oz) dried cranberries

100g (3½oz) candied peel, shop-bought or homemade (page 202), chopped

100g (3½oz) currants

4 dates (pitted) (100g/3½oz), halved

100ml (3½fl oz) whiskey, plus extra for serving

100g (3½oz) ground almonds

2 cooking apples, such as Bramley or Granny Smith, grated (do not peel)

Finely grated zest and juice of 1 lemon

6 tbsp golden syrup

10 whole, blanched (skinned) almonds

200g (7oz) butter, chilled and grated

180g (6oz) soft dark brown sugar

4 eggs, beaten

230g (8oz) gluten-free flour or 250g (9oz) self-raising flour, sifted

½ tsp baking powder

¼ whole nutmeg, finely grated

½ tsp ground cinnamon

ingredients continue overleaf

When I was growing up, our Christmas pudding would vary a little each year. My mum didn't use exact quantities of anything, and I liked that each year was different. I'm like that myself, adding a little more or less of some ingredients some of the times. I love the not-so-traditional cranberries in this recipe, which give the pudding a delightfully zingy flavour.

In a saucepan, gently simmer the dried fruit in the whiskey for 3 minutes. Remove from the heat, cover and leave for at least 1 hour.

Mix the ground almonds, apples and lemon zest and juice together in a bowl.

Set out two (1 litre/1¾ pint) pudding basins or deep, heatproof bowls, preferably ceramic. Pour 3 tablespoons of golden syrup into each of the pudding basins and arrange 5 almonds and a few pieces of soaked fruit decoratively in the golden syrup.

Using a wooden or metal spoon, mix the grated butter, brown sugar and eggs together in a large bowl. Add the flour, baking powder, nutmeg and cinnamon and mix together thoroughly. Spoon into the pudding basins and flatten out. Gently bang the bowls on the work surface to release any air bubbles.

Cut two rounds of parchment paper to fit neatly over the top of each, then cut out two more rounds about 5mm (¼in) wider than the rim of the basin. Place them over the basins and tie with a long piece of string under the lip of the bowl and over the top again. Tie at the other side to make a handle.

Place each basin in a large saucepan and carefully pour hot water around them to come three-quarters of the way up the sides. Cover and steam for 3 hours, keeping the water in the saucepan topped up all the time.

Remove the basins from the water and allow to cool. Remove the top paper lid and cover with a new one. Store in a cool place.

recipe continues overleaf

FOR THE WHISKEY ORANGE CREAM

100ml (3½fl oz) double cream

1–2 tbsp icing sugar, sifted

2 tbsp Irish whiskey

Finely grated zest of 1 small orange

Reheat by steaming for 1 hour in the same way as above. Meanwhile, make the whiskey orange cream. Whip the cream until just stiff and fold in the icing sugar, whiskey and orange zest.

To serve, turn the puddings out onto a large plate. Pour a little whiskey over and ignite. Serve with the whiskey orange cream.

Candied peel

Vegetarian

Makes about 1.1 litres (1¾ pints)

Preparation time: 30 minutes plus 24 hours soaking

Cooking time: 4 hours plus 30 minutes cooling

5 oranges

5 lemons

5 grapefruit

1 tsp salt

1.25kg (3lb) caster or granulated sugar

You can use the mixture of fruit suggested here, or just fifteen of the same fruit.

Cut the fruit in half and squeeze out the juice. (Reserve the juice for another use, perhaps homemade lemonade.) Put the peel into a large bowl, add the salt and cover with cold water. Leave to soak for 24 hours.

Next day, throw away the soaking water, put the peel in a large saucepan and cover with fresh cold water. Bring to a boil, cover and simmer very gently for about 3 hours, or until the peel is soft. It should mash between the tips of your fingers easily when it is cooked. Remove the peel from the pan and discard the water. Scrape out any remaining flesh and membrane from inside the cut fruit, using a teaspoon, leaving the white pith and rind intact.

In a clean large saucepan, dissolve the sugar in 1 litre (1¾ pints) of water, then bring to a boil, stirring to dissolve the sugar. Add the peel and simmer gently for 30–60 minutes until it looks shiny and translucent ('candied') and the syrup forms a thread when the last drop falls off a metal spoon. Remove from the heat and allow to stand for 20–30 minutes to cool slightly.

Put the candied peel into sterilised glass jars (see page 188) and pour the syrup over. Cover and store in a cold place or in the fridge. It should keep, stored like this, for at least 3 months. You can chop or slice the candied peel as you need it.

St. Stephen's Day muffins

Vegetarian

Makes 6 muffins

Preparation time: 20 minutes

Cooking time: 25 minutes

Ready in 1 hour

1 egg

6 tbsp milk

25g (1oz) butter, melted

2 tbsp sherry, Irish whiskey or brandy

125g (4½oz) leftover Christmas Pudding (page 200), broken into lumps

125g (4½oz) plain flour

1 tsp baking powder

½ tsp mixed spice

75g (3oz) caster sugar

Icing sugar, for dusting

What better way to use up any bits of leftover Christmas pudding than with these festive and delicious muffins? They are divine with a cup of coffee or tea and can be frozen.

Preheat the oven to 180°C/350°F/Gas Mark 4. Line a 12-hole muffin tin or 24-hole mini muffin tin with paper cases.

Whisk the egg in a bowl, then add the milk, melted butter, sherry and the pieces of Christmas pudding.

Sift the flour, baking powder and mixed spice into another bowl. Add the caster sugar and mix well. Make a well in the centre, add the wet ingredients and mix together until a soft, lumpy batter forms.

Spoon the mixture into the paper cases and bake for 20–25 minutes, until the muffins feel springy to the touch.

Allow to cool in the tin for a few minutes, then remove from the tin and place on a wire rack to cool completely. Dust with icing sugar to serve.

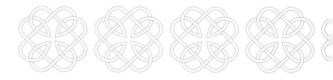

Irish coffee meringue roulade

Vegetarian

Serves 6–8

Preparation time: 30 minutes

Cooking time: 25–30 minutes

Ready in 2 hours

A little vegetable oil, for greasing

4 egg whites

225g (8oz) caster sugar

1 tbsp instant coffee powder

FOR THE FILLING

425ml (15fl oz) whipping cream

1 tsp instant coffee powder

1 tbsp sifted icing sugar, plus extra
for dusting

2 tbsp Irish whiskey

This Irish coffee roulade is quite a grown-up dessert. It's decidedly wintery and I like to make it when there's not much fresh fruit around. Of course, we know just how well whiskey and coffee go together, and this dish is perfect served with small Irish Coffees (page 210).

Preheat the oven to 180°C/350°F/Gas Mark 4. Line a 23 x 33cm (9 x 13in) Swiss roll tin with foil, folding the sides up to make a frame 4cm (1½in) high and squeezing the corners together. Brush lightly with vegetable oil.

Put the egg whites in the spotlessly clean bowl (stainless steel is best) of an electric food mixer (or use a hand-held electric beater) and whisk until soft peaks form.

Add the sugar all in one go (but if using a hand-held beater, add the sugar in stages) and whisk at full speed for 4–5 minutes, until stiff peaks form. Using a large metal spoon, fold in the instant coffee firmly and quickly. Spoon the meringue into the prepared tin and smooth with a spatula.

Bake for 15–20 minutes, until faintly browned and firm to the touch.

Allow the meringue to cool for a few minutes, then turn out onto a sheet of foil (slightly bigger than the roulade), carefully turning it upside down onto the sheet and gently removing the foil on the bottom. Allow to cool completely.

To make the filling, whip the cream until it forms soft peaks, then fold in the instant coffee, icing sugar and whiskey. Spread the coffee cream over the meringue, leaving the long edge nearest to you free of cream for about 4cm (1½in).

Holding the foil closest to you, roll up the roulade away from you and leave it in the foil until you are ready to serve (it will hold neatly here for a couple of hours in the fridge).

When ready to serve, unwrap the roulade and gently push it onto a serving dish using a spatula. Dust with icing sugar and serve immediately.

Irish coffee cups

Vegetarian

Serves 4

Preparation time: 30 minutes

Cooking time: 25–30 minutes

Ready in 2 hours

125g (4½oz) butter, softened

125g (4½oz) soft light brown sugar

2 eggs

1 tbsp coffee essence (ideally Camp or Irel brand)

125g (4½oz) plain flour

1 tsp baking powder

150ml (5fl oz) double or whipping cream, softly whipped, to serve

FOR THE SAUCE

125g (4½oz) caster sugar

6 tbsp water

150ml (5fl oz) double or whipping cream

4 tbsp Irish whiskey

Warm coffee cakes served in teacups with a whiskey sauce and whipped cream, these make a smart and playful dessert, perfect for a dinner party, because both the cakes and sauce can be made ahead of time. The cakes are better if made on the same day, but the sauce can be made up to a couple of days ahead. Reheat the sauce in a saucepan and reheat the cakes in the oven (preheated to 130°C/250°F/Gas Mark ½) for 10 minutes or just until warmed through. Serve with Irish Coffee (page 210).

Preheat the oven to 180°C/350°F/Gas Mark 4 and butter the insides of four small ovenproof teacups or four 6cm (2½in) diameter ramekins, if you intend to tip the cakes out of them for serving.

Cream the butter until soft in a large bowl or with an electric food mixer fitted with the paddle attachment. Add the brown sugar and beat until the mixture is light and fluffy.

Whisk the eggs with the coffee essence in a small bowl for just a few seconds until mixed, then gradually add to the creamed butter mixture, beating all the time. Sift in the flour and baking powder and fold in gently to combine.

Divide the mixture among the teacups or ramekins and place these in a deep-sided ovenproof dish or roasting tin. Pour boiling water into the dish so it comes to halfway up the sides of the cups.

Bake for 25–30 minutes, until the centre of each cake is springy to the touch.

While the cakes are baking, make the sauce. Combine the caster sugar and water in a saucepan and bring to a boil, stirring to dissolve the sugar as the mixture heats up. Turn the heat up to high and continue to boil, but without stirring, until the syrup becomes a deep golden caramel colour. Cook the sauce just to the point when it starts smoking. (If it's not cooked enough you won't get a strong enough caramel flavour, but if overcooked it will taste slightly bitter.) You may need to swirl the pan, rather than stirring the mixture, toward the end of caramelising to ensure it cooks evenly.

recipe continues overleaf

Turn down the heat and immediately stir in the cream and whiskey, taking care as it may bubble and spit; then set aside. You may need to whisk it for a few seconds over low heat to help the caramel dissolve into the cream and whiskey.

When the cakes are done, remove from the oven and allow to cool for a couple of minutes. Place on saucers or serving plates, or tip them out onto warm plates if you prefer. To serve, pour a tablespoon of the warm whiskey sauce over each, then top that with a spoonful of softly whipped cream.

Irish coffee

Vegetarian

Serves 1

Preparation time: 5 minutes

35ml (1¼fl oz) Irish whiskey (Paddy's, Powers or Jameson)

1½ tsp brown sugar

Hot coffee

Softly whipped cream

Irish coffee was invented by Joe Sheridan at what was then Shannon Airport in 1942. The story goes that on a particularly stormy evening, one plane was lucky to land, and Joe Sheridan, the chef at the airport's restaurant, wanted to make a drink to warm them through. He added Irish whiskey to a sweetened coffee with cream. One of the passengers asked if they were drinking Brazilian coffee, and Joe replied that it was Irish coffee. The drink is now universally popular and still served all over Ireland.

The trick with Irish coffee is that there must be enough sugar in the coffee to support the weight of the cream. If there's not enough sugar, the cream sinks to the bottom. The cream shouldn't hold a stiff peak, but should hold a very soft peak.

Pour the whiskey into a cup and stir in the brown sugar. Top up with coffee, leaving a space of 1cm (½in) from the rim of the cup to the top of the coffee, and stir to dissolve the sugar. Dip a spoon into hot or boiling water, then use that spoon to add the cream to the coffee – it will slide gently off the spoon.

Little hot after-dinner shots

Vegetarian

Serves 8

Preparation time: 5 minutes

Cooking time: 3 minutes

200ml (7fl oz) brandy or whiskey

200ml (7fl oz) Stock Syrup
(see below)

8 tbsp softly whipped cream

Merrilees Parker, a wonderful British cook, made something similar to this when I appeared with her on the television show Great Food Live. I like to serve this after a winter dinner party. It is nicely luxurious – a little like Irish coffee, only without the coffee!

Pour the brandy and syrup into a saucepan and heat very gently; do not boil. Divide among eight little glasses. Dip a spoon into boiling water and use to spoon on the cream, allowing it to slide off the spoon and sit on top of the sweet brandy or whiskey. The cream should not sink. Serve immediately.

Stock syrup

Vegetarian

Makes 150ml (5fl oz)

Preparation time: 5 minutes

200g (7oz) caster or granulated
sugar

200ml (7fl oz) water

This basic sugar syrup has many uses, including sweetening cocktails and poaching fruit. It keeps indefinitely, and it is very handy to have some on hand.

Combine the sugar and water in a saucepan and bring slowly to a boil, stirring to dissolve the sugar. When the sugar has dissolved, boil for 2 minutes and allow to cool.

Steamed ginger treacle pudding

Vegetarian

Serves 6

Preparation time: 30 minutes

Cooking time: 1½ hours

Ready in 2 hours

125g (4½oz) butter, diced and softened, plus extra for greasing

4 tbsp black treacle

4 tbsp ginger syrup (from the stem ginger jar)

110g (4oz) soft light brown sugar

2 eggs

150g (5oz) self-raising flour, sifted

2 tbsp milk

75g (3oz) stem ginger, very finely chopped

Ice cream, softly whipped cream or Custard (page 182), to serve

This pudding is really just a hug in a bowl. The glorious steamed pudding is made perfectly sweet with the toffeelike flavour of treacle and the gentle heat of ginger. You can buy stem ginger in syrup online if you can't find it elsewhere. Alternatively, you can use crystallised ginger in the cake batter and then golden syrup in place of the ginger syrup in the treacle mix.

Butter a 1 litre (1¾ pint) pudding basin or deep, heatproof bowl, preferably ceramic. Mix the treacle and the ginger syrup together and pour into the bottom of the basin.

Cream the butter and brown sugar together by hand or with an electric food mixer fitted with the paddle attachment until light and fluffy. Beat in the eggs, one at a time. Fold in the flour and add in the milk. Stir in the stem ginger and spoon the mixture into the pudding basin to fill it two-thirds of the way up, smoothing the top with the back of the spoon. (The treacle will come up the inside of the basin, so be careful not to mix it into the cake mixture.)

Butter a piece of greaseproof paper and fold a pleat across the centre. Cover the basin with the paper, butter side down, and secure with string under the lip of the basin (see page 200). Place in a steamer with a tight-fitting lid and simmer over low heat for 1¼–1½ hours, until the top of the pudding is firm to the touch and a skewer inserted into the middle comes out clean. Remember to top up the water in the steamer, if necessary.

Alternatively, if you don't have a steamer, sit the pudding basin on an upturned saucer in the bottom of a large saucepan. Pour enough boiling water to come halfway up the sides of the basin and cover with a tight-fitting lid, then cook for the same length of time. Again, remember to keep the water topped up all the time.

Remove the pudding basin from the steamer, carefully loosen the pudding by running a spatula around the inside of the basin and invert onto a warm serving plate (one that is wider than the top of the basin). The treacle sauce will ooze down the sides of the pudding. Spoon over any sauce remaining in the basin and serve with ice cream, whipped cream or custard.

Dark sticky gingerbread

Vegetarian

Makes 1 loaf

Preparation time: 20 minutes

Cooking time: 55 minutes

Ready in 1 hour 40 minutes

60g (2½oz) butter

75g (3oz) golden syrup

50g (2oz) molasses or black treacle

110g (4oz) plain flour

25g (1oz) self-raising flour

1 tsp bicarbonate of soda

1 heaped tsp ground ginger

1 tsp ground cinnamon

1 tsp freshly grated nutmeg

1 tsp freshly ground black pepper

100g (3½oz) caster sugar

Pinch of salt

120ml (4½fl oz) milk

1 egg, beaten

50g (2oz) crystallised ginger, finely chopped

FOR THE SYRUP

80g (3oz) caster or granulated sugar

80ml (3fl oz) water

1 tsp finely grated fresh ginger

FOR THE TOPPING (OPTIONAL)

200g (7oz) icing sugar, sifted

Juice of ½ lemon

This classic teatime cake can be served warm with cream as a dessert or sliced and buttered at any time. The flavour is quite intense, and it's the kind of treat that is immensely satisfying. It stays deliciously moist and has a lovely mixture of different spices so will keep very well. Divine with a cup of coffee.

Preheat the oven to 170°C/325°F/Gas Mark 3. Line a 13 x 23cm (5 x 9in) loaf tin with parchment paper.

Melt the butter, golden syrup and molasses in a small saucepan over low heat. Set aside.

Sift the flours, bicarbonate of soda, ginger, cinnamon, nutmeg and pepper into a large bowl. Stir in the sugar and salt. Add the milk and egg and mix until smooth. Gradually add the melted butter mixture, stirring until well incorporated. Fold in the chopped crystallised ginger. The mixture will be runny. Pour into the prepared loaf tin.

Bake for 50–55 minutes, until risen and firm to the touch, and a skewer inserted into the middle comes out clean. Do not open the oven to test before the bread has baked for at least 45 minutes.

After the gingerbread has been baking for about 40 minutes, make the syrup. Combine the sugar, water and grated ginger in a small saucepan and simmer for 10 minutes. When the gingerbread is done, remove from the oven and prick all over with a fine skewer. Pour over the hot syrup, then place the loaf tin on a wire rack to cool for 20 minutes. Remove the cake from the tin and place on a wire rack to cool completely.

To make the topping, mix together the icing sugar and lemon juice in a small bowl until thick and smooth. Spread carefully over the top of the cake with a spatula or a table knife, allowing some icing to drip over the edges.

Brown bread ice cream

Vegetarian

Serves 6–8

Preparation time: 30 minutes

Cooking time: 15 minutes

Ready in 12 hours

100g (3½oz) chopped Brown Soda Bread (page 227) or Brown Yeast Bread (page 230)

50g (2oz) soft brown sugar

¼ tsp ground cinnamon

150ml (5fl oz) double or whipping cream

2 eggs, separated

1 tbsp rum (optional)

125g (4½oz) granulated sugar

100ml (3½fl oz) water

Pinch of cream of tartar

It may seem strange, but this Victorian invention is a divine ice cream. It's a wonderful way of using our great Irish bread, whether it's brown soda bread or brown yeast bread. The crumbs are mixed with sugar and caramelised in the oven. The deeply flavoured sweet nuggets are then stirred into the rich ice cream. This is perfect on its own or with a butterscotch, caramel or chocolate sauce (page 220).

This recipe is particularly useful as it doesn't require an ice cream machine; you simply stir the cream into an Italian meringue, then freeze it overnight. The ice cream it makes is very light and doesn't need to soften before scooping.

Preheat the oven to 200°C/400°F/Gas Mark 6.

Place the bread in a food processor and whiz for 30–60 seconds to form coarse breadcrumbs. Add the brown sugar and cinnamon and pulse for a few times just to mix. Spread out on a baking tray and toast in the oven for about 10 minutes, until well browned. Remove from the oven and set aside to cool.

Whisk the cream until soft peaks appear, then mix in the egg yolks and rum (if using) and set aside.

Combine the granulated sugar and water in a saucepan and heat slowly, stirring to dissolve the sugar. Increase the heat to high and bring to a boil. Boil fiercely for 5 minutes, until the syrup thickens and the last drops on a spoon dipped into it form a sort of thread. Meanwhile, using an electric whisk, whisk the egg whites with the cream of tartar until stiff. Still whisking, gradually pour in the hot syrup in a thin stream and continue to whisk until the mixture is cool, glossy and stiff, 4–5 minutes. Add the whipped cream mixture along with the caramelised breadcrumbs and fold until mixed through.

Transfer the mixture to a container with a lid, cover and place in the freezer. Freeze overnight before serving.

Dark chocolate sauce

Vegetarian

Makes 175ml (6fl oz)

Preparation time: 5 minutes

Cooking time: 5 minutes

75g (3oz) chopped dark chocolate

100ml (3½fl oz) double or whipping cream

Very quick to make, this hot chocolate sauce is the ultimate in sinfulness – perfect drizzled over any ice cream, especially the Brown Bread Ice Cream (page 218). Although it keeps in the fridge for several weeks, I challenge you to leave it there for that long.

Melt the chocolate in a heatproof bowl sitting over a saucepan of gently simmering water. Whisk in the cream to make a smooth sauce. Keep warm in the bowl until ready to serve.

Breads and biscuits

Fresh bread, whether soda or yeast, is a pleasure to have, both to serve with other food and for the wonderful aromas that fill the kitchen. Soda bread is the quintessential Irish bread. It has long been made in home kitchens and restaurants everywhere and is still to this day. While soda bread is quick to put together, I also adore bread made with yeast, though it takes a little more time.

This chapter also has a number of different recipes for biscuits and fruit breads, the sweet treats that I often bake to serve with tea or coffee.

Soda bread

Vegetarian	
Makes 1 loaf	
Preparation time: 10 minutes	
Cooking time: 45 minutes	
Ready in 1 hour 10 minutes	

450g (1lb) plain flour, plus extra for dusting

1 tsp caster sugar

1 tsp bicarbonate of soda

1 tsp salt

350–425ml (12–15fl oz) buttermilk or soured milk (see tip, page 228)

This traditional Irish loaf is one of the fastest bread recipes to make.

Preheat the oven to 230°C/450°F/Gas Mark 8.

Sift the flour, sugar, bicarbonate of soda and salt into a large bowl. Make a well in the centre and pour in most of the buttermilk, leaving about 50ml (2fl oz) in the measuring jug. Using one hand with your fingers outstretched like a claw, bring the flour and liquid together, adding more buttermilk if necessary. Don't knead the mixture, or it will become heavy. The dough should be soft, but not too wet and sticky.

When the dough comes together, turn it onto a floured work surface and bring it together a little more. Pat the dough into a round about 4cm (1½in) thick and cut a deep cross in it. Place on a baking tray.

Bake for 15 minutes. Turn down the heat to 200°C/400°F/Gas Mark 6 and bake for 30 minutes more. When done, the loaf will sound slightly hollow when tapped on the bottom and be golden in colour. I often turn it upside down for the last 5 minutes of cooking. Allow to cool on a wire rack.

Brown soda bread

Vegetarian

Makes 1 loaf

Preparation time: 10 minutes

Cooking time: 45 minutes

Ready in 1 hour 10 minutes

225g (8oz) wholemeal flour

225g (8oz) plain flour

1 tsp salt

1 tsp bicarbonate of soda

50g (2oz) mixed seeds, such as sesame, pumpkin or sunflower or golden linseeds (optional)

25g (1oz) butter, softened (optional)

1 egg

375–400ml (12–14fl oz) buttermilk or soured milk (see tip, page 228)

Soda bread is quintessentially Irish and still made fresh in kitchens every day. It is so easy to make and is absolutely at its best eaten the day it's made. The bicarbonate of soda (called 'bread soda' in Ireland) is the leavening agent, reacting with the buttermilk to produce bubbles of carbon dioxide and leaven the bread. You can eat brown soda bread with many different foods, but it is especially good with smoked salmon and mackerel and with hard cheese and chutney.

Preheat the oven to 220°C/425°F/Gas Mark 7.

Sift together the flours, salt and bicarbonate of soda in a large bowl and mix in the seeds (if using). Add the butter (if using), and rub into the flour mixture with your fingertips until it resembles breadcrumbs. Make a well in the centre.

In another bowl, whisk the egg with the buttermilk and pour most of the liquid into the flour mixture. Using one hand with your fingers outstretched like a claw, bring the flour and liquid together, adding more of the buttermilk mixture if necessary. The dough should be quite soft, but not too sticky.

Turn onto a floured work surface and gently bring the dough together into a round about 4cm (1½in) thick. Cut a deep cross on top and place on a baking tray.

Bake for 15 minutes. Turn down the heat to 200°C/400°F/Gas Mark 6 and bake for 30 minutes more. When done, the loaf will sound slightly hollow when tapped on the bottom. Remove from the baking tray and place on a wire rack to cool.

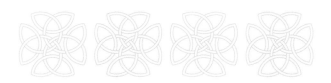

Cheesy soda scones

Vegetarian

Makes about 16 scones

Preparation time: 10 minutes

Cooking time: 20 minutes

Ready in 50 minutes

450g (1lb) plain flour

1 tsp salt

1 tsp bicarbonate of soda

1 tbsp chopped fresh herbs, such as rosemary, thyme, sage, parsley or chives

400ml (14fl oz) buttermilk or soured milk (see tip)

75g (3oz) grated Cheddar or Gruyère cheese

All children love playing with dough, and with this Irish soda bread dough you can be as creative as you like. I often leave out the herbs; sometimes I leave out the cheese and replace the herbs with a handful of chopped milk or dark chocolate, or even raisins or dried cranberries. These scones can be cut into any shapes that your little ones like, though if handled and kneaded too much, they will get slightly tough.

Preheat the oven to 250°C/475°F/Gas Mark 9. Flour a baking tray.

Sift the flour, salt and bicarbonate of soda into a bowl. Mix in the herbs. Make a well in the centre. Pour in all the buttermilk at once. Using one hand, with your fingers outstretched like a claw, stir in a full circular movement from the centre to the outside of the bowl to form a dough. The dough should be soft, though not too wet and sticky.

When the dough comes together, turn it out onto a well-floured surface. Pat the dough until it is about 2cm (¾in) thick. Cut into sixteen round or square shapes and place on the prepared baking tray. Generously sprinkle each scone with the grated cheese.

Bake for about 15 minutes, until golden and sounding hollow when tapped on the bottom. Turn the oven down to 200°C/400°F/Gas Mark 6 after 10 minutes if they are already golden. Remove from the baking tray and place on a wire rack to cool slightly before serving.

Variations

To make chocolate chip soda scones, omit the cheese and replace the herbs with 75g (3oz) of chopped dark or milk chocolate or chocolate chips. You could also add an egg to the buttermilk and 1 tablespoon caster sugar to increase the richness. It's also delicious with 100g (3½oz) raisins or dried cranberries.

Rachel's tip

To make your own soured milk, gently heat the milk (the quantity required for the recipe) until warm. Remove from the heat, add the juice of ½ lemon and leave at room temperature overnight. If you are allergic to dairy products, this recipe works well with soy milk or rice milk soured in the same way.

Ballymaloe brown yeast bread

Vegetarian	
Makes 1 loaf	
Preparation time: 10 minutes	
Cooking time: 1 hour	
Ready in 1¾ hours	

A little vegetable oil for greasing

450g (1lb) wholemeal flour or 400g (14oz) wholemeal flour plus 50g (2oz) strong white flour

1 tsp salt

1 tsp black treacle or molasses

425ml (15fl oz) lukewarm water

25g (1oz) fresh yeast or 2 x 7g (¼oz) sachets fast-action yeast

1 tbsp sesame, poppy or sunflower seeds (optional)

This brown yeast bread is a version of Doris Grant's no-knead brown bread as made by my grandmother-in-law, Myrtle Allen. Because it isn't kneaded, this bread only takes minutes to make and is full of the divinely nutty whole-grain flavour. If you'd like a slightly lighter loaf, you can substitute strong white flour for some of the wholemeal flour. You can also add a sprinkling of seeds for nutty flavour and added nutrition.

This bread has a distinctive flavour that works well with other strong flavours and is the perfect bread to serve with smoked fish.

Preheat the oven to 220°C/425°F/Gas Mark 7. Grease a 23 x 13cm (9 x 5in) loaf tin with vegetable oil. Make sure all of the ingredients are at room temperature.

Mix the flour with the salt. In a small bowl or Pyrex measuring jug, mix the treacle with 150ml (5fl oz) of the lukewarm water and add in the yeast. Let it sit for a few minutes in a warm place to allow the yeast to start to work. After 4 or 5 minutes, it should have a creamy, slightly frothy appearance.

When the yeast is ready, stir and pour it, with all the remaining water, into the flour to make a loose sloppy dough. The mixture should be too wet to knead. Put the mixture into the greased loaf tin. If using the seeds, sprinkle them over the dough now. Lay a tea towel over the top of the tin. Leave on your work surface to rise to the top of the tin. It will take from 5–25 minutes to rise, depending on the temperature of the kitchen and the dough itself. Remove the towel and pop the loaf in the centre of the oven. Look at the loaf after 20 minutes; if it is a deep brown, reduce the oven temperature to 200°C/400°F/Gas Mark 6. After 50–60 minutes, the loaf should look nicely browned and sound hollow when tapped. Remove from the oven, take out of the tin and place on a wire rack to cool.

If you'd like a thicker crust, remove the loaf from the tin 10 minutes before the end of baking and place directly on an oven rack to bake for the last 10 minutes.

Wholemeal honey bread

Vegetarian

Makes 2 loaves

Preparation time: 30 minutes

Cooking time: 40 minutes

Ready in 4 hours

450ml (14fl oz) warm water

3 tbsp honey

1 tbsp active dry yeast or fast-action yeast or 40g (1½oz) fresh yeast

600g (1lb 5oz) strong white flour

300g (11oz) wholemeal flour

2 tsp salt

100g (3½oz) butter, cut into 1cm (½in) cubes

Making yeast bread from scratch is becoming a lost art, but it is the perfect thing to do with your children – to teach new skills and to have fun. This is a simple and tasty bread, and once you have mastered it, you'll want to move on to other flavours and combinations.

In a small bowl, mix the warm water with the honey; add the yeast and let stand for 5 minutes until slightly frothy.

Combine the flours in a big mixing bowl or in the bowl of an electric food mixer fitted with the dough hook attachment and mix in the salt. Rub in the butter. Pour most of the frothy liquid into the flour and mix to form a dough. If it's too dry and feels floury, add a little more warm water; if it feels very wet and sticky, add a little more flour.

Knead by hand on a floured work surface or in the mixer for about 10 minutes (it may only take 5 minutes in the mixer), until the dough is smooth and springy. Place in a large oiled bowl, cover with cling film and leave in a warm spot for 2–3 hours, until it has doubled in size and does not spring back when you push your finger into the dough.

Knock back the dough by punching it down in the bowl (my children love this bit!) and knead on the floured surface for 1 minute. Allow to rest on the work surface, covered with a tea towel, for 5 minutes.

I usually shape the dough into two round or oval loaves but, of course, you can make individual rolls if you wish (you will get about 20 rolls). Slash the loaves four or five times over the top with a sharp knife (I don't do this with rolls). Do make sure you flatten the loaves and rolls to about 4cm (1½in) in height because they will rise.

Preheat the oven to 200°C/400°F/Gas Mark 6.

Place the loaves (or rolls) on a floured baking tray, sprinkle with flour, cover with a tea towel and let rise in a warm place until doubled in size, about 45 minutes. The dough has risen enough when it does not spring back when you push your finger onto it.

Remove the tea towel and bake the loaves for 30–40 minutes (bake rolls for 10–15 minutes), until a loaf sounds hollow when tapped on the bottom. Cool on a wire rack.

Spotted dog

Vegetarian

Makes 1 loaf

Preparation time: 10 minutes

Cooking time: 45 minutes

Ready in 1 hour 10 minutes

450g (1lb) plain flour, plus extra for dusting

1 tsp bicarbonate of soda

1 tsp salt

1 tbsp caster sugar

110g (4oz) sultanas, raisins or currants (or a mixture)

1 egg

400ml (14fl oz) buttermilk or soured milk (see tip, page 228)

This is a rich white soda bread with dried fruit added to make it 'spotted'. A real family favourite of ours, it's divine served straight from the oven, cut into slices and smothered in butter and jam or toasted and topped with cheese.

Preheat the oven to 220°C/425°F/Gas Mark 7. Lightly dust a baking tray with flour.

Sift the flour, bicarbonate of soda and salt into a large bowl. Stir in the sugar and dried fruit.

In a separate bowl, beat together the egg and buttermilk. Make a well in the centre of the dry ingredients and pour most of the buttermilk mixture (leaving about 50ml/2fl oz in the bowl).

Using one hand with your fingers outstretched like a claw, bring the flour and liquid together moving your hand in circles around the bowl, adding a little more of the buttermilk mixture if necessary. Don't knead the mixture, or it will become too heavy. The dough should be soft, but not too wet and sticky.

Once it comes together, turn onto a floured work surface and bring together a little more. Pat the dough into a round, about 6cm (2½in) in height, and cut a deep cross in it, from one side of the loaf to the other. Transfer to the prepared baking tray.

Bake for 10 minutes, then reduce the oven temperature to 200°C/400°F/Gas Mark 6 and bake for another 30–35 minutes, until the bread is golden and sounds hollow when tapped on the bottom. I often turn the loaf upside down for the last 5 minutes of baking to help crisp the bottom. Allow to cool on a wire rack before cutting into thick slices to serve.

Variation
Spotted dog scones: Preheat the oven to 230°C/450°F/Gas Mark 8. Make the spotted dog dough as above but flatten into a round about 3cm (1in) in height. Cut into scones using a biscuit cutter or knife and bake for 15–20 minutes.

Barmbrack (báirín breac)

Vegetarian

Serves 8

Preparation time: 30 minutes

Cooking time: 45 minutes

Ready in 1¾ hours

225g (8oz) strong white flour, plus extra for dusting

2 tbsp mixed spice

¼ tsp salt

25g (1oz) butter, plus extra for spreading

1 x 7g (¼oz) sachet fast-action yeast

50g (2oz) caster sugar

150ml (5fl oz) milk

1 egg, beaten

200g (7oz) mixed dried fruit, either ready-mixed or your own mixture of sultanas, raisins and currants

25g (1oz) chopped mixed candied peel, shop-bought or homemade (see page 202)

Barmbrack is a traditional Irish sweetened bread not dissimilar to the Welsh bara brith. In Gaelic it's known as báirín breac, or 'speckled loaf', due to the way the dough is dotted with raisins. When barmbrack was baked for Halloween, the tradition was to add to the cake mixture a pea, a stick, a piece of cloth, a coin and a ring. Each item had a special significance for the person who discovered it in their slice of cake. The person who received the pea wouldn't marry that year; the stick meant an unhappy marriage; the cloth indicated poverty and the coin riches; while the person who found the ring would wed within the year. Nowadays it's usually just a ring that's added to the batter. The cake is delicious toasted and buttered and, if not immediately consumed, will keep for about 10 days.

This is a relatively quick recipe for barmbrack because it uses fast-action yeast, requiring the dough to rise only once.

Butter the sides and the bottom of a 23 x 13cm (9 x 5in) loaf tin.

Sift the flour, mixed spice and salt into a large bowl and add the butter, yeast and sugar. Beat together by hand or in an electric food mixer fitted with a dough hook attachment.

Warm the milk just until lukewarm, then add to the flour mixture along with the egg. Mix until the dough comes together, then knead using an electric food mixer fitted with a dough hook attachment, or tip the dough out onto a well-floured work surface and knead by hand (don't worry, this is supposed to be a wet dough). Knead for 8 minutes by hand or for 5 minutes in the mixer. Add the dried fruit and mixed peel and knead for another 2 minutes to mix them in.

Put the dough into the prepared loaf tin, cover with a light tea towel or napkin and leave to rise in a warm place (by a radiator, for instance, or a sunny window) for 1 hour, or until doubled in size.

Meanwhile, preheat the oven to 180°C/350°F/Gas Mark 4.

Remove the covering and bake for 45 minutes, or until deep golden brown on top. When you think the loaf is ready, gently loosen the sides with a spatula and tip it out of the tin. If it's fully cooked, it should sound slightly hollow when you tap it on the bottom and feel springy when you lightly squeeze the sides. Place it on a wire rack to cool.

Slice up the loaf and serve either fresh or toasted, and buttered.

Chocolate, raisin and almond biscuits

Vegetarian

Makes 16–18

Preparation time: 15 minutes

Cooking time: 10 minutes

Ready in 35 minutes

150g (5oz) butter

150g (5oz) plain flour

½ tsp bicarbonate of soda

50g (2oz) ground almonds

50g (2oz) steel-cut oats (stone or porridge oats)

50g (2oz) raisins

50g (2oz) soft brown sugar

50g (2oz) caster or granulated sugar

100g (3½oz) dark chocolate, cut into chunks

1 large egg yolk or 2 small ones

The oats in these biscuits give them a wonderful and ever so slightly chewy texture. The ground almonds make them moist, and the slight bitterness of the dark chocolate is offset by the sweetness of the sugar and raisins. These are refined enough to serve after dinner with coffee, but I don't need an excuse to eat two or three!

Preheat the oven to 180°C/350°F/Gas Mark 4.

Melt the butter in a saucepan over medium heat. Remove from the heat and set aside to cool.

Sift the flour and bicarbonate of soda into a bowl, then stir in the ground almonds, oats, raisins, brown sugar, caster or granulated sugar and chocolate.

Mix the egg yolk with the cooled melted butter. Add to the dry ingredients and stir to mix everything together. Use your hands to make walnut-size balls and arrange slightly apart from each other on two baking trays. Gently flatten slightly.

Bake for 8–10 minutes, until golden. Allow to cool for a few minutes, then use a metal spatula or palette knife to transfer them to a wire rack to cool completely.

Ginger biscuits

Vegetarian

Makes about 50

Preparation time: 10 minutes

Cooking time: 15 minutes

Ready in 35 minutes

225g (8oz) butter, softened

225g (8oz) caster sugar

150g (5oz) golden syrup

1 egg

450g (1lb) plain flour

1 tbsp ground ginger

1 tsp bicarbonate of soda, sifted

These biscuits were my dad's favourites, so they were one of the first things I baked when I was younger. This recipe makes quite a lot, but you can freeze the unbaked biscuits and cook from frozen. They'll take 5–10 minutes longer.

Preheat the oven to 180°C/350°F/Gas Mark 4.

Combine all the ingredients in a food processor and pulse a few times until they come together to form a soft dough. If you don't have a food processor, cream the butter in a bowl, then add in the sugar and golden syrup and beat together. Then stir in the rest of the ingredients to form a soft dough.

Use your hands to form walnut-size balls of the dough and place them 6cm (2½in) apart on a baking tray (no need to grease it). You will need two or three baking trays, or you can make them in two or three batches.

Bake for 10–15 minutes, or until golden brown. Remove the baking trays from the oven and allow to cool for a few minutes, then use a metal spatula or palette knife to transfer them to a wire rack to cool.

Shortbread

Vegetarian

Makes 25

Preparation time: 15 minutes

Cooking time: 10 minutes

Ready in 35 minutes

150g (5oz) plain flour

50g (2oz) caster or granulated sugar

100g (3½oz) butter, softened

This shortbread is quick to make, crisp and buttery, and wonderfully versatile. It is a great go-to recipe to serve plain, with tea or coffee, or with puddings such as Fluffy Lemon Pudding (page 178) and Carrageen Moss Pudding (page 197).

Preheat the oven to 180°C/350°F/Gas Mark 4.

Combine the flour and sugar in a mixing bowl. Rub in the butter and bring the whole mixture together to form a stiff dough. Do not add any water.

Roll out the dough to a thickness of about 5mm (¼in) and cut into shapes. Place carefully on a baking tray about 3cm (1in) apart.

Bake for 6–10 minutes, or until pale golden. Using a spatula, carefully transfer the shortbread onto a wire rack to cool.

Variations
Add 1 teaspoon ground ginger, or 1 teaspoon ground cinnamon, or finely grated zest of 1 orange, or finely grated zest of 1 lemon, or 2 tablespoons sifted cocoa powder or 2 teaspoons dried lavender.

Wholemeal shortbread

Vegetarian

Makes about 20

Preparation time: 15 minutes

Cooking time: 10 minutes

Ready in 35 minutes

75g (3oz) wholemeal flour

75g (3oz) plain flour

100g (3½oz) butter, softened

50g (2oz) caster or granulated sugar

My boys love making these as they can choose whatever shapes they like. They are great for birthday parties and lunch boxes. They are also good sandwiched together with raspberry jam!

Preheat the oven to 180°C/350°F/Gas Mark 4.

Combine all of the ingredients in a food processor and whiz until the mixture almost comes together and resembles coarse breadcrumbs. Tip onto the work surface and bring it together with your hands. If you are not using a food processor, rub the butter into the combined flour and sugar in a bowl and bring together with your hands.

Sprinkle your work surface with a little flour (wholemeal or white) and roll out the dough to a thickness of about 5mm (¼in) or roll it between two pieces of cling film. Using a biscuit cutter, cut into whatever shapes you wish or just cut simply into squares with a knife. Transfer to a baking tray (no need to grease or line it) spaced about 3cm (1in) apart.

Bake for 6–10 minutes depending on the size, until they are pale golden and feel firm on top. Using a spatula, remove carefully and cool on a wire rack.

Oaty shortbread

Vegetarian

Makes about 40

Preparation time: 15 minutes

Cooking time: 20 minutes

Ready in 45 minutes

275g (10oz) rolled oats

100g (3½oz) plain flour

150g (5oz) caster sugar

½ tsp bicarbonate of soda

1 tsp salt

225g (8oz) butter, softened

These lovely biscuits are surprisingly delicate even though they contain hearty oats. My children love them, and I often put them in their school lunch boxes – though sweet, the addition of oats makes them good and nutritious (just don't tell them!).

Preheat the oven to 180°C/350°F/Gas Mark 4.

Whiz the oats in a food processor until they are quite fine. Then add the remaining ingredients and whiz again until the dough comes together.

Roll out the dough on a floured work surface to a thickness of about 5mm (¼in). Cut into squares, circles or shapes with biscuit cutters and place on baking trays (no need to grease or line) spaced about 3cm (1in) apart.

Bake for 15–20 minutes, until pale golden and slightly firm. Using a spatula, carefully transfer to a wire rack to cool. These will keep for 5–6 days in an airtight container, and they freeze well, too.

Oatcakes

Vegetarian

Makes about 30

Preparation time: 15 minutes

Cooking time: 20 minutes

Ready in 45 minutes

200g (7oz) rolled oats

¼ tsp salt

¼ tsp baking powder

25g (1oz) butter, softened

1 tbsp extra virgin olive oil

100ml (3½fl oz) boiling water

A handful of finely ground oatmeal, for rolling

Mixed seeds, such as sesame, millet, poppy or golden linseeds, freshly ground black pepper or salt crystals, such as Maldon, for sprinkling (optional)

Oatcakes are perfect for anyone with wheat intolerance. Few things rival them for serving with cheese. They aren't strongly flavoured – some people put spices in their oatcakes but I don't think that's necessary. The oatcakes should only play a supporting role while the cheese itself is the star of the show.

Preheat the oven to 170°C/325°F/Gas Mark 3.

Combine the oats, salt and baking powder in a food processor and whiz for 2 minutes until it is finer in texture and looks similar to ground almonds. Add the butter and whiz until combined.

With the motor running, pour in the olive oil and boiling water, stopping frequently to check if the dough is coming together. Don't let it get too wet.

Turn the dough out onto a work surface dusted with finely ground oats and knead just to bring it together. Roll the dough out as thinly as possible, to a thickness of 2–3mm (1/16–1/8in). Sprinkle the dough with seeds or grind some pepper or sprinkle some salt on top, if you wish. Give the dough another light roll to make sure the seeds stay on.

Using a 5–8cm (2–3¼in) round cutter or a knife, cut the dough into rounds, triangles or squares. You can re-roll and use the scraps as well. Place on baking trays (don't oil or butter) spaced about 4cm (1½in) apart.

Bake for 15–20 minutes, until lightly browned on the edges and crisp. Transfer to a wire rack to cool.

Wholegrain sesame seed cheese crackers

Vegetarian

Makes 25–30

Preparation time: 10 minutes

Cooking time: 45 minutes

Ready in 1 hour 10 minutes

100g (3½oz) wholemeal flour

100g (3½oz) plain flour, plus extra for dusting

3 tbsp sesame seeds

¾ tsp salt

½ tsp baking powder

25g (1oz) butter

1 tbsp single cream

4–5 tbsp water

These nutritious crackers are full of wholesome seeds as well as whole wheat. They have a lovely sesame flavour that works best with strongly flavoured cheeses.

Preheat the oven to 150°C/300°F/Gas Mark 2. Lightly flour a baking tray.

In a bowl, mix together the flours, sesame seeds, salt and baking powder. Rub in the butter and cream until the mixture resembles loose breadcrumbs. Add just enough water to form a firm dough.

Dust a work surface and the dough with flour. Roll out the dough to a thickness of about 2mm (⅟₁₆–⅛in). Prick all over with a fork, then cut into rounds measuring about 6cm (2½in) in diameter using a biscuit cutter, or cut into squares using a knife or pastry wheel. Transfer to the prepared baking tray spaced about 5cm (2in) apart.

Bake for about 45 minutes, or until lightly browned and quite crisp. Remove from the oven and transfer to a wire rack to cool.

Index

This edition first published in 2013 by Collins.

This book includes recipes and images first published in *Rachel's Favourite Food at Home* (2006), *Rachel's Food for Living* (2007), *Rachel's Diary 2009* (2008), *Bake* (2008), *Home Cooking* (2009), *Entertaining at Home* (2010), *Easy Meals* (2011) and *Cake* (2012).

HarperCollins*Publishers*
77–85 Fulham Palace Road
London W6 8JB

www.harpercollins.co.uk
www.harpercollins.com

10 9 8 7 6 5 4 3 2 1

A catalogue record for this book is available from the British Library.

ISBN: 978-0-00-723762-3

Printed and bound in China by South China Printing Co Ltd.

Collins